UNMUTED:
The Cost of Silence and the Courage to Speak

Dr. Michele D'Amico

Dedication

For all the women who have been and are still silenced. For the women who refuse to stay silent, and for the men who choose to stand with them.

For my daughter, Olivia and my sister, Barb. Two of the smartest and most inspiring women I know. Your encouragement reminded me, every step of the way, why this book had to be written. And to my brother-in-law, Dan, who continues to show through both his words and his heart what it means to stand with women as equals. And to Robert who has always believed in me. I love you all beyond words.

To my mom and my nana, who are no longer with us but who taught me, each in her own way, to stand in my truth. I am forever grateful.

Acknowledgments

Writing this book was not a solitary act. It was shaped by every woman who sat across from me in coaching sessions, every conversation where someone whispered, "Me too," and every story of courage that reminded me why this work matters.

To the women who bravely shared their experiences of being muted and unmuted — thank you for trusting me with your stories. Your voices are the backbone of these pages, and I carry them with deep respect.

To the friends and colleagues who would not let me give up when the words felt too heavy, your faith in me kept this book alive.

To my inner circle — you know who you are — thank you for reading early drafts and holding space for my frustration and joy along the way.

To my editor, who guided this book with a steady hand, thank you.

And to you, the reader. May it embolden you to claim your voice, to help others claim theirs and amplify those who cannot speak for themselves.

Contents

Story

I once set up a meeting with a male client with the goal of introducing him to a long-time contact of mine — someone I also consider a good friend. She is the public works director for a coastal community, a position that carries tremendous responsibility.

During our conversation, he repeatedly referred to her (never in her presence) as "that gal." Each time, I responded by saying "the public works director," hoping to elevate the language and remind him of her professional stature. He continued to say "gal."

Needless to say, I decided not to move forward with any introductions. This "gal" is a highly skilled, hardworking public works director, and she deserves to be addressed as such — not reduced to a casual, dismissive label that ignores her role and accomplishments.

INTRODUCTION: WHY UNMUTED?

"The most common way people give up their
power is by thinking they don't have any."
— Alice Walker

Do you feel the tectonic cultural shift? Women are rising, speaking, and claiming the space that has too long been rationed to us. Around the world, we see it in grassroots movements and in viral hashtags. Once-silent dinner tables are alive with conversations that refuse to be muted. The old model of power is fraying, and this time, the backlash is severe. We seem to take one step forward and two steps back again and again. For many women, the instinct to stay small, agreeable, and quiet is hard to completely eradicate. We've learned to measure our words. To question our instincts. To shrink ourselves enough to fit in.

But silence has a cost. Playing small has a cost. It costs us our power, our connection, our sense of agency. It disconnects us from our own truth, and too often, it disconnects us from each other. We internalize the misogynistic belief that powerful women are threatening. That to lead is to invite scrutiny and judgment. That to use our voices is to risk being misunderstood, dismissed, ignored, or worse, hated.

Power and voice are inseparable. You cannot claim one without the other. Voice is how we know ourselves. It is how we connect, how we name the world around us, and how we change it. But many of us were never taught how to trust our voices, let alone use them. We were taught to modulate or mute our voices to make them more palatable for men. And when we did speak up, we were told we were too loud, too emotional, too much.

This book is a call to unmute.

Being unmuted is not about speaking louder. It is about speaking. And when you do, speak truth. It's about reconnecting to the voice within. The one that reflects what you have always known. When we strip away the conditioning, the performance, the layers of "should" that have kept us from fully inhabiting our lives, we find our voices and use them. This book is not only for women in boardrooms or on stages. It's for women in classrooms, kitchens, hospital rooms, small businesses, art studios, community centers, and every space in between. It is also for the men who support us. It's for any woman who has ever felt the tug to stay quiet when she wanted to speak. Any woman who has ever questioned her right to take up space. Any man who wants the other half of the population to enjoy the same right to speak truth as he has.

What you'll find here is not a how-to guide to becoming louder. It is an invitation to connect to yourself. Through stories, reflections, cultural insights, and practical tools, I hope to help you recognize how and where you learned to mute your voice so you can reclaim your agency, courage, and emotional honesty. In doing so, you will redefine what power can look and feel like and use your voice to create change in your life and the world.

I hope this is a journey of individual transformation and a collective evolution. When women speak fully, fiercely, and freely, systems begin to shift. Cultures begin to heal. Futures begin to open.

We are not waiting to be given power. We are remembering we had it all along.

Thanks for taking this journey with me.

Story

Early in my career, I was a single woman working for as a Public Relations Director for a health care facility in Louisiana — very much a "who's your daddy" environment. Over time, I learned that my male counterparts were earning more than I was, even though we held the same roles (and, truthfully, I was often working harder).

I decided to address it directly. I went to the head of Human Resources, respectfully and appropriately, and asked for a salary review. Not even a raise — just a review. His response is burned into my memory: "What does a young girl like you need more money for?" The message was clear. In his eyes, I should find a husband to take care of me rather than expect fair pay for my own work.

Although I did eventually receive raises later in my career, the results of that particular review were never shared with me. The experience remains a vivid reminder of how bias and dismissal once openly shaped workplace culture — and how far we still have to go.

Chapter 1:

Shifting The Power Paradigm

"I want every girl to know that her voice can change the world."
— *Malala Yousafzai*

P ower. It's a word that many women struggle with. Too much of it, and you're intimidating. Too little, and you're overlooked. In many environments, women are walking a tightrope trying to lead without being labeled, trying to speak without being silenced, trying to succeed without being seen as "too much."

But the issue isn't women. It's the outdated paradigm of power itself and not one of our creation. We struggle to claim our power because that is what we have been taught.

Many of us grew up watching a very specific kind of leader. Strong. Certain. Commanding. Male. These were the leaders who dominated boardrooms and headlines. They led with authority and control in a hierarchical structure, in other words from the top down. They rarely showed emotion (except for anger, which was acceptable), never said "I don't know," and often succeeded by outshouting or outmaneuvering the competition.

This model was designed by and for a male-dominated power structure that expected obedience, and disdained collaboration, and for a world that rewarded aggression, and scorned empathy.

A world where leadership was about status and control, not service and compassion.

And yet, this is the model many of us were expected to follow.

Telling women to 'speak up' without dismantling the systems that silence them is gaslighting.

I grew up in the 60s and 70s. As a young girl in the 60s, children were meant to be seen and not heard – especially little girls. My father passed away when I was four and my mother suddenly became a single mother of three children under the age of five. I was sandwiched between two boys. At that time, a woman could not buy a home or have a bank account without her husband's signature.

The world around me wasn't built for strong little girls. Hell, it wasn't built for girls. But I had a secret weapon. My paternal grandmother (nana) was a strong female influence until she died when I was 16. She came over from Italy by herself at a very young age. She ran a grocery store with my grandfather until his death and later turned it into a restaurant/bar. She was strong and confident, compassionate and smart, and spoke her mind when it was not fashionable to do so. Though we never discussed gender roles, I felt her power and it stuck with me.

I was drawn to powerful women in television and movies. There was a popular show called *The Avengers* starring Diana Rigg as the beautiful, powerful Emma Peel, a woman who could be neither silenced nor sidelined. She was a huge influence on me. Oh, how I cried when she left the show! Barbara Stanwyck, Elizabeth Taylor, Katherine Hepburn, and, of course, Bette Davis and Mary Tyler Moore also stand out as women who broke the rules and played strong women on the screen. These women weren't voiceless and they weren't powerless even within the confines of their era.

SHE WAS **WARNED.** NEVERTHELESS, SHE **PERSISTED.**

Photo courtesy of Lucy Knisley (Artist/Author)

After my father died, I withdrew. I didn't speak out. I was timid—a sudden introvert. If you ask

11

anyone who knows me today, they would be shocked! I was treated very differently than my brothers were. Sports were a no-no for girls, but baby dolls were acceptable. Later, my mother remarried and had two more children, a boy and a girl. My role was to be a second mom to the younger kids, to babysit and take care of household duties like making the beds, vacuuming, and doing the dishes, while my brothers maybe were asked to take out the garbage, a stereotypical male chore that involved physical strength and little time commitment.

I often felt very alone in my family. On some level, I knew I was different but couldn't put the knowing into words. It was clear to me early in life that I could not possibly stay in my small town. Don't get me wrong—I loved my family. Especially my younger brother and sister. Even though I was tasked with caring for them much of the time, they gave me purpose and an unconditional love that was intoxicating and fulfilling.

As I got older, I rebelled. I felt powerless and struggled to understand and accept the unfairness of what it meant to be a girl. I understood intuitively that I was not permitted to express myself and ask for what I needed, things boys were encouraged to do. The double standard was intolerable and is the root of the double bind with which women are very familiar

The Double Bind

Here's where it gets complicated: when women try to emulate this traditional form of power, they often face backlash. Studies show that women who assert themselves in leadership roles are more likely to be perceived as abrasive, unlikable, or too aggressive. Also, ironically, too emotional. Assertiveness in men, on the other hand, is seen as a positive and even sought after trait.

So, we find ourselves in a bind:

- Be assertive, but not too assertive and make it clear you will acquiesce if needed.
- Be confident but stay humble.

- Speak up, but not too much, and don't be loud.

The result? Exhaustion. Self-doubt. Imposter syndrome. Or in my case, anger and frustration. And a lingering question in the back of our minds: *Do I really belong here?*

I knew early on that I didn't belong in the small township outside of Pittsburgh, Pennsylvania where I grew up. I did not want to stay geographically close to my family. Everything seemed too small, confining, and just downright unfair. To this day, any double standard angers me. By the time I got to middle school, I simply couldn't play the role I was given any longer and rebelled. This began a very long journey for me with drugs, alcohol and sex. That might be a story for another time!

The Cost of Playing a Role

To succeed in spaces built for someone else's definition of leadership and someone else's definition of womanhood, many women end up playing a role. We perform leadership. We perform life. We study how to sound "executive," how to be "likable," how to appear effortless, agreeable, composed. We shrink or self-edit to make others comfortable. We adjust our tone, our ambition, even our joy. And we pay for it with our energy, our well-being, and, maybe worst of all, our authenticity.

It doesn't just happen at work. It happens in friendships, in motherhood, in dating, in caregiving, in social media feeds where we feel the pressure to be both strong and soft, assertive but never aggressive, powerful yet never intimidating and always, always attractive...but not too attractive! These expectations can be so deeply internalized, we begin to believe the performance is who we should be, and maybe even who we really are.

When we lead or live like someone we're not, it creates a disconnect, not just with others, but with ourselves. We begin to doubt our own instincts. We question whether our voice, our style, or our story is valid. Guilty as charged! The cognitive dissonance is overwhelming and dangerous. And, over time, we may stop showing up fully at all.

When power looks like something we're not, we either play small or adopt a role.

Naming the Disparity

Before we can redefine power, we have to name the disparity. We have to acknowledge that the traditional paradigm wasn't built with women in mind. Not just in leadership, but in life. From boardrooms to bedrooms, classrooms to caregiving roles, we've inherited models that expect us to perform rather than belong. To accommodate rather than assert. To carry more while asking for less.

And we've learned to navigate these systems quietly, often blaming ourselves when we don't feel at ease inside them. We question our confidence, our competence, our capacity, when the truth is that the structure was never designed for us to thrive. The "ideal leader," the "good mother," the "perfect woman." These roles were written by men who chose not to take our complexity, our contradictions, or our full humanity into consideration.

We're not the problem, the model was never built with us in mind, and it's time for a redesign.

We don't need to "fix" women to fit life or leadership. We need to fix the systems, expectations, and definitions to reflect reality. We need a new paradigm.

Traditional power taught us that control equals strength, that influence must be won through domination, and that certainty should override curiosity. It showed up—and still does—in hierarchies, at home, at work, in politics, where decisions were made by men at the top and questioning those decisions was discouraged, or even punished, especially if you were a woman. It taught us that power was a finite resource: if someone else had it, you didn't.

For women, traditional power often came with qualifiers. Women were expected to walk a narrow line. Be confident but not intimidating; be strong, but still soft; speak up, but don't be loud. Be visible but not commanding, competent but deferential. This version of the power permitted (and yes, I mean permitted) to women left little room for nuance, emotional intelligence, collaboration, or compassion. It was a performance of authority shaped by masculinity, whiteness, and capitalism, and it rewarded those who could conform to its mold. Regrettably, we are seeing a return to this model in the current climate.

This hasn't been the model in all cultures. Many indigenous and matrilineal societies offer a different perspective, one where power was rooted in relationship, wisdom, and contribution to the collective.

In the Iroquois Confederacy, for example, clan mothers held significant political power. These women were responsible for selecting and deposing male leaders (sachems), ensuring that those in authority acted with integrity and in service to the people. Their leadership wasn't about dominance; it was about stewardship and accountability. Power was measured not by how much you controlled, but by how well you listened and protected the well-being of the group.

Similarly, in parts of pre-colonial West Africa, such as among the Akan people of Ghana, women served as queen mothers, leaders who advised chiefs, managed land, and played crucial roles in conflict resolution and spiritual guidance. Their influence was not symbolic; it was institutional. They exercised power through their wisdom, not by suppressing others.

What these histories remind us of is that the paradigm of power as control is not universal or inherent in human DNA—it's cultural. It is a byproduct of colonization, patriarchy, and capitalism, and therefore not inevitable. Once we see that, we can reimagine power on our own terms.

What we know now is this: power isn't just about who holds the mic, it's about who feels free to speak. Real power creates room, not scarcity. It uplifts rather than controls. We've learned that relational power rooted in trust, inclusion, and authenticity is not only more humane, it's also more effective.

We see this shift happening in real time. When New Zealand Prime Minister Jacinda Ardern stepped down in 2023, she said, "I no longer feel I can do the job justice." It wasn't a sign of weakness; it was a radical act of leadership grounded in self-awareness. I wonder if any of our male leaders would do the same…Ardern's tenure was marked by compassionate crisis response, emotional intelligence, and moral clarity. She led through presence, not posturing, offering the world a powerful model of leadership grounded in care, not control.

The future of power is not dominance. Though lately, things seem dismal at times, I still choose to believe that the future of power is shared agency. It's collective voice. It's leadership that centers integrity over ego, collaboration over coercion, and courage over compliance.

We don't have to keep replicating the old model. There are other ways. There have always been other ways.

We see the evolution of power in grassroots movements like *Ni Una Menos* ("Not One [Woman] Less"), which began in Argentina in 2015 as a response to the epidemic of femicide and gender-based violence. What started as a protest turned into a continental movement, a tapestry of women's voices woven across Latin America, calling not just for justice, but for a redefinition of power itself. Powered by digital organizing and the raw testimonies of survivors. The movement used social media to document injustice, organize rallies, and pressure governments for legal and cultural reform.

Think of it like a quilt, stitched from different fabrics, textures, and histories. Each square represents a voice, a region, a lived experience. No single piece tells the whole story, but together, they create something resilient, beautiful, and impossible to ignore. *Ni Una Menos* isn't powered by hierarchy, it's powered by connection.

This same collective model is reflected in U.S.-based grassroots efforts like the #*Say Her Name* campaign or Indigenous-led efforts to raise awareness in a campaign called *Missing and Murdered Indigenous Women and Girls* (MMIWG). These movements also center the voices of those historically silenced, using shared leadership, storytelling, and community resilience to challenge systems of erasure and violence.

They show us that real power doesn't need to dominate to be effective. It needs to include. It needs to listen. And it needs to support rising together.

Vision for Redefining the Power Paradigm

Imagine a new model of power, one that doesn't require you to shrink, perform, or constantly walk a tightrope. A model built on collaboration instead of competition, compassion instead of control, and authenticity instead of endless accommodation.

Redefining power means creating space for leadership that reflects who we really are—complex, bold, resilient, and unapologetically human—and humane. It invites us to stop asking, *"How can I fit in?"* and start asking, *"How can I lead in a way that feels true?"*

To reclaim power is to untangle it from the definitions we've inherited and instead root it in courage, collaboration, and values. I'm not advocating that we abandon our ambition. I'm talking about aligning ambition with authenticity. Adding the word ambition to our vocabulary, not as a bad word but to help us reclaim it on our own terms.

Women don't lack power. But we've often been taught to pursue someone else's version of it or to restrain it by lowering our voices.

Redefined power asks deeper, more courageous questions, questions that shift our lens from control to connection, from performance to presence.

- *What does power look like when it's in service of people, not ego?*

  When power is used to uplift rather than dominate, it creates space for others to speak, to rise, to belong. It stops being a spotlight and becomes a shared light. In this version of power, collaboration isn't a soft skill, it's a strategy. And generosity is not a weakness, it's a force.

- *What happens when leadership is measured by trust, not volume?*

  Leadership isn't how loud we speak, but how deeply we listen. Actively listening with our hearts, ears, and head leads to true understanding and builds trust. When we build trust instead of creating fear, we invite loyalty, not compliance. Whether you're managing a team, raising a child, or supporting a friend, the same principle applies. People are more willing to grow with you when they feel safe in your presence.

- *How does it feel to live and lead from wholeness instead of performance?*

  When we stop shapeshifting to meet other people's expectations, we reclaim enormous amounts of energy previously expended unnecessarily. We stop bracing and start belonging. Living from wholeness means we act as our authentic selves. We no longer compartmentalize our strengths, silence our needs, or wear masks to make others comfortable. It means we show up fully, imperfectly, and unapologetically.

Playing real, not small—in the workplace, our relationships, our communities means we're not shrinking to fit outdated molds or someone else's ideal. We're showing up as we are, so we can completely reshape what power looks like.

As a woman, I have struggled on and off through life with this idea of being 100% authentic. It's not an easy fix. It's scary and it can make you feel exposed. Even as a child, I felt a struggle inside of me. I hated being told who I was supposed to be and rebelled against it, but as a child and young adult, there wasn't much room to find out *who* I was let alone *be* that person. I've learned a few things along the way.

How the Old Paradigm Shows Up Today

If you're wondering whether the old definitions of power are still shaping your life, ask yourself:

- Do I measure my success by how much I do, rather than how fulfilled I feel?
- Do I feel guilty when I say no?
- Do I downplay my wins to avoid being seen as "too much"?
- Do I push through exhaustion rather than ask for support?
- Do I silence my voice in spaces where it matters most?

The old model isn't just something we've seen, it's something we've absorbed. It's a shape strange to us that we try to force ourselves into. Recognizing where that old model still controls us is the first step toward change.

Small Acts of Defiance: Where Redefining Power Begins

Redefining power doesn't require a grand public declaration or a sweeping life overhaul. It often begins in small, defiant moments. Use your voice. Choose yourself in places where you once chose silence.

It begins when you:

- Say no without explanation
- Ask for help and refuse to apologize for needing it
- Let yourself take up space in rooms that were never intended for you
- Lead with empathy, even when yours is not the loudest voice in the room.
- Celebrate your wins without shrinking them to make others comfortable

Each of these moments is a quiet rebellion against outdated expectations and a step toward speaking with your own voice.

Looking back now, I can see that every small act of rebellion, saying no when I was expected to say yes, choosing college when I was told it was a waste, daring to believe there was something more for me, wasn't just defiance. It was the beginning of reclaiming my power by finding my voice. Becoming not the version of me that I had been handed, but the version I chose for myself. And that's where real leadership begins, with the courage to stop performing and start becoming.

And like any voice that's been silenced or ignored, when I first began to use mine, I started quietly. But with every decision to choose myself, to choose what felt authentic over what felt expected, my true voice grew louder, steadier, and more certain. It still took me years to really own it.

As you're reading this book, I invite you to stop performing and start becoming. To rediscover the power of your own voice, not the one the world taught you to use, but the one you were born with. Because when you find your voice, you don't just change your story. With your own voice in your mouth, you change the way you lead, live, love, and show up for yourself and others. And that's where real change begins.

Finding your voice is the starting point for reclaiming your power. For too long, women have been taught to soften our edges, lower our volume, and second-guess our instincts. But real leadership and real freedom begin the moment you choose to trust your own voice, even if it shakes. Speaking up isn't always easy, but it is the first bold act of stepping into your power.

Not everyone will like it when we speak up. But I've made peace with that, and you can too.

Your voice is more than words; it's the embodiment of your truth. Actions count as voice too. It's how you show the world who you are and what you stand for. When you finally allow yourself to be fully seen and heard, something extraordinary happens.

You stop waiting for permission and start becoming the person you've been waiting for—the leader, the doer, the creator, the powerful one living her truth.

I'm not talking about being loud. I'm talking about standing firm in your truth, using your voice with intention and clarity, and leading from a place of authenticity. When you lead with the power of your own voice, you not only change how others see you, you change how you see yourself.

Story

The first time I met my counterpart in my current role, our conversation was a bit contentious. My industry is still largely white and male, and he fit that profile perfectly. We had been tasked with hiring a new team member. His suggestion was to hire a young man who had just married and had a child because, in his words, "he would work hard." I could not resist replying, "Are we discussing 80's movie themes right now?"

Fast forward to a company-wide video conference with all of my counterparts and our CEO. Cameras were on. The CEO was sharing sobering news about losses and the state of the business. In the middle of this serious conversation, my counterpart sent me a private message: "You look unhappy." The unspoken message was clear - I should smile.

For the remainder of the meeting, I made sure my face stayed completely neutral, perhaps even a little less than "happy," just to make the point that my expression was not his to manage.

Chapter 2:

The Roots of Silence

"A woman with a voice is by definition a strong woman.
But the search to find that voice can be remarkably difficult."
– Melinda French Gates

Before we can reclaim our voices, we need to understand the forces that silenced them. Silence doesn't begin in the boardroom, the classroom, or the relationship. It begins at birth. Silence is taught in subtle messages, our social conditioning, and deeply ingrained beliefs.

Many of us were taught to be "good girls" through lessons both overt and subliminal. We were conditioned into silence one 'be nice' at a time. We absorbed, without consciousness of its implications, that being "good" meant quiet, polite, obedient, and agreeable. We learned to raise our hands, wait our turn, not interrupt, not take up too much space, literally and figuratively. We learned that being liked was safer than making ourselves heard, and also more likely if we were quiet. That it was better to avoid conflict than to speak the truth, especially if what we had to say went against the grain, aka the patriarchy. Being accommodating was the price of acceptance. We learned this lesson as children, when acceptance and love were critical to our security and growth, which meant our early survival was linked to being obliging and compliant.

These lessons were rarely taught outright, but we absorbed them easily from sideways glances, cold reactions to our exuberance, compliments that rewarded our silence ("She's so well-behaved!"), and reprimands that punished our fire ("Don't be so bossy."). They were reinforced by the media we consumed, the role models we were told to emulate, the invisible rules that governed girlhood and continued into womanhood.

By the time we reached adolescence, the roots of silence had already taken hold. We learned to edit our opinions, defer to others, and apologize for having needs. We internalized the belief that our worth was tied to how little we asked for and how much we gave. We learned to doubt our instincts, to override our discomfort, and to mistrust our own wisdom.

Silence, then, became our path to survival.

And for many of us, it still is.

In the workplace, raising a concern might label us as difficult. So, we remain silent. In relationships, expressing our needs might be met with resistance, dismissal, or ridicule. So, we remain silent. In families, generational roles and expectations often linger, and acceptance and belonging hinge on our living up to them. So, we remain silent. Even silence within ourselves. The stories and feelings we don't examine, the truths we tuck away, the dreams we defer are the result of these awful lessons.

I want to be clear: this silence is not our fault. It is a response to a culture that has rarely welcomed our voices. A cultural status quo that has benefited from our silence. My intention is to reclaim context, not to assign blame. To see clearly so we can choose differently.

The roots of silence run deep, but they can be extricated.

Silence is passed down not just through personal experience but through generational, cultural, and systemic patterns. Generationally, we inherit silence from the women who came before us—mothers, grandmothers, aunts—who were likely taught that keeping quiet was the key to survival, respectability, or love. Some were silenced through trauma or circumstance and passed down the belief, spoken or unspoken, that it's safer not to speak at all. Men have played a significant role in mandating women's silence to ensure the continuation of the patriarchal systems they depend on. Through inherited expectations of authority, discomfort with emotion, or the unchallenged norms that equate male dominance with social and family stability, even "good" men perpetuate women's silence, often unconsciously. These beliefs are passed down as well, shaping the dynamics we all grow up in.

Culturally, silence is shaped by expectations around gender, race, class, and ability. In many cultures, girls are raised to be deferential, modest, and self-sacrificing, while boys are encouraged to speak up, take charge, and lead. For women of color, the intersection of race and gender often compounds the pressure to stay silent or to speak only in ways deemed acceptable by dominant norms. These patterns aren't confined to one generation. They are embedded into the stories we're told, the behaviors we model, and the institutions we navigate.

In South Asian communities, for instance, a woman's silence may be seen as a sign of virtue and dignity. Upholding family honor is often emphasized, and questioning elders or expressing dissatisfaction can be viewed as disrespectful. Girls may grow up learning that obedience is not just expected, it's revered. Speaking out can carry social consequences that extend beyond the individual, impacting the entire family's standing in the community. It's a heavy load to carry.

Systemically, silence is reinforced through education, media, policy, and power structures that continue to reward conformity over authenticity. From textbooks that erase female contributions, to workplace cultures that penalize assertiveness in women, to legal systems that fail to protect us or even listen to our voices when we have the guts to use them to right a wrong. These mechanisms work together to uphold the status quo.

In fact, modern research shows that gender bias continues to shape how women's voices are received in courtrooms, board-rooms, and beyond. For example, until the late 19th century in English common law, married women were often prohibited from testifying independently in court due to laws like coverture, which legally bound their identities to their husbands'. This limitation reflected a broader belief that women's words carried less weight than men's.

We still see this today in the U.S and around the world. Women witnesses, especially in cases involving sexual assault or domestic violence are subjected to heightened scrutiny. Studies reveal that they are more likely to be perceived as less credible or overly emotional, particularly when their testimonies challenge dominant narratives or social expectations. According to the American Bar Association, gender bias in legal proceedings remains a serious concern, meaning that female attorneys and witnesses must meet higher standards of judgment and credibility.

Mock jury studies reinforce this. Male witnesses are often seen as more trustworthy than women, particularly when women show emotion or express dissent. This reveals a systemic bias that does not just silence women but actively undermines their truth.

Within these systems, many of us also internalized what we might call invisible contracts, unwritten rules about what it means to be "good," "strong," or "successful." These contracts vary across families, cultures, and communities, but they often share a common thread: compliance over courage, silence over truth, pleasing over pushing back.

To be "good" might mean never rocking the boat, never disappointing others, never choosing yourself. We see this when men are esteemed for extolling their achievements and the work it took to get where they are, whereas women who articulate their own achievements, are thought to lack humility and even shamed for doing so. To be "strong" might mean never needing help, never showing emotion, never breaking down. To be "successful" might mean checking all the boxes others set out for you, even if they don't align with who you are.

These contracts were not negotiated. They guided us without our participation in their creation. They were inherited through observation, expectation, and reward. And because they often come wrapped in love, tradition, or security, it can be difficult to see them for what they are: agreements we never consciously signed, but that shaped how we show up or shrink in the world.

Identifying silence and naming it are the first steps of unmuting. And every time we name it, we loosen its grip. Every time we speak the truth of what was withheld, ignored, or erased, we create space for a new story.

Naming the silence opens the door to awareness. Awareness brings to the surface what has long been buried. The recognition that the silence we carry is not a personal failing, but a cultural inheritance can usher in change. What has been learned can be unlearned.

Your voice is not lost. It is waiting.

And when we listen closely enough, we can still hear it beneath the silence, steady and strong, ready to rise.

Ambition Without Apology

For generations, women were taught to downplay ambition, to be modest, deferential, grateful. Ambition in men was admired; in women, it was often questioned, pathologized, or punished. We've been taught that wanting more makes us selfish, that striving makes us "too much."

But ambition is not a dirty word. Ambition is a declaration that your life matters, that your vision matters, that your impact matters. It's the drive to contribute, to create, to grow. And it deserves to exist without apology, especially when it's rooted in values and aligned with purpose.

Ambition without apology means refusing to shrink your goals to make others comfortable. It means making space for your own dreams, even if no one else understands them yet. As women, we can step fully into ourselves without stepping on others.

This unapologetic ambition can be traced through the stories of women who have changed the world, not by waiting for permission but by boldly envisioning something more. Whether it's the scientist in a male-dominated lab, the entrepreneur who launches a mission-driven startup, or the mother who redefines success on her own terms, ambition is a throughline that refuses to be erased.

We can look as far back as 1869 to figures like Annie Turnbo Malone who was born to formerly enslaved parents in Illinois. From an early age she was fascinated by chemistry, and she began experimenting with ways to create healthier hair care products for Black women. At a time when the products on the market were damaging and demeaning, she saw possibility. In the early 1900s she began selling her own formulas door to door, demonstrating how her products could transform hair and restore dignity.

By 1902 Malone had moved to St. Louis and founded the Poro Company, which quickly grew into a national powerhouse. Through her company and the creation of Poro College, she not only manufactured products but trained thousands of women in both hair care and business. For many, this was the first chance at financial independence. She gave women not just income, but professional identity and pride in a society that worked to deny both.

Her story is often overshadowed by that of her onetime protégé, Madam C.J. Walker, who later founded the Madam C.J. Walker Manufacturing Company in 1910. Walker built her own thriving empire and created an army of "Walker Agents" who carried her vision across the country. Yet it was Malone's pioneering breakthroughs, her chemistry, and her business model that made that path possible. At her peak, Malone was one of the wealthiest Black women in America, a philanthropist and visionary who insisted that unmuted ambition could transform not just an individual life but an entire community.

While Malone was building economic power, another woman was fighting for survival and dignity in an entirely different realm. Susan La Flesche Picotte was born in 1865 on the Omaha Reservation in Nebraska, just a few years before Malone. As a young girl she watched a Native woman die because a white doctor refused to treat her. That moment lit a fire she would never extinguish. In 1889 she became the first Native American woman in the United States to earn a medical degree.

She returned to her reservation and treated thousands of patients, traveling mile after mile on horseback in brutal weather with little rest and almost no pay. She carried medicine with her and cared for people in their homes. In 1913, she achieved a milestone no one thought possible: the creation of the first hospital on Native land, funded through her own relentless advocacy and determination. Though she died in 1915 at just fifty years old, she left behind a legacy of healing, resilience, and uncompromising courage.

Malone and La Flesche came from different worlds, but their stories converge on the same truth: unmuted women reshape history. Malone opened economic doors where none had existed. La Flesche brought dignity and survival to her people when the world denied their worth. Both refused silence. Both insisted on creating futures larger than themselves.

Or we can look all around us, to the women rebuilding after divorce, reimagining careers in midlife, returning to school after raising children. Ambition doesn't always announce itself with a loud bang. Sometimes, it whispers I am still here. I still want more.

Ambition without apology is not a rejection of others. It's a reclamation of self.

Unapologetic ambition also means knowing that your purpose doesn't require explanation and trusting that your vision is valid even if it's not yet realized. Your desires are not a burden, they are beacons.

To be ambitious, as a woman, is to defy centuries of conditioning. Ambition says: I choose expansion over shrinking, vision over compliance, and voice over silence. We need only to look at Congresswoman Alexandria Ocasio-Cortez or Jasmine Crockett to see two women who expand and choose voice over silence. Their very presence in the political arena is an act of defiance against a system that was not designed for them, and their insistence on being heard reminds us that ambition is not arrogance, it is survival and transformation.

And when we do that collectively, we don't just change our own lives, we redefine power and ambition.

A New Definition of Strength and Success

The traditional model of strength is glorified stoicism. It convinced us that strength meant never breaking, never showing weakness, never asking for help. Success, in that same model, was defined by accumulation of titles, wealth, approval, and accolades, many of which were withheld from women. It was measured by how much you could do and how little you seemed to need.

But that model doesn't hold up anymore, if it ever really did. It creates isolation, disconnection, and personal hardship. It's not just unsustainable; it's untrue.

Real strength is not the absence of struggle. It's the capacity to move through it without abandoning yourself. Strength means allowing yourself to feel fully, to be human in the face of pressure, and to keep going. Not because you're unbreakable, but because you are rooted in something deeper.

I know this is true in my life. I have struggled mightily for many years. For a while, even after I thought I found my voice, I was knocked down again and again, losing my confidence and being unable to speak my truth. I'm still not great at asking for help, but

I strive to embrace that part of me because I know it's critical to my ability to stand in my power. I'm working on it!

And success? It doesn't have to mean being the busiest person in the room or checking the boxes someone else set. Success can mean alignment, joy, impact, and freedom. It can mean saying no to what drains you and yes to what feeds your spirit. It can mean choosing presence over perfection, and purpose over performance.

A woman who knows her worth without needing validation, who defines success on her own terms and builds a life that reflects it is most definitely a powerful force.

When we redefine strength as wholeness and success as authenticity, we don't lower the bar, we raise the standard. We shift from striving to being. We rise with intention. We build lives and leadership that are sustainable, soulful, and deeply real.

And in doing so, we make it safer for other women to do the same. That is powerful and something I am passionate about. I have a daughter, and while she, like the rest of us, stands on the shoulders of the women who have come before, I never want her to question her voice or her own power.

Every time we claim our own definition of strength, we loosen the hold of a culture that told us we had to be superhuman, while also being less than.

And every time we claim a version of success that honors our truth, we build a new world, for ourselves, and for the ones who come next.

Voice is not just the ability to speak; it's the ability to be heard and taken seriously. Voice is how we claim space, express truth, and shape the world around us. When our voices are suppressed through fear, cultural expectation, or systemic bias, our power is diminished.

Throughout history, women's voices have been silenced or dismissed, not because they lacked value, but because they carried too much of it, and were thus seen as a threat to the status quo. We are seeing this in real time with the rise of the Manosphere and the Incel culture where men blame women and feminism for their inability to have a relationship or to find a submissive woman. To reclaim our voices, then, is to reclaim our agency. Every time a woman names her needs, shares her story, or challenges injustice, she reclaims a piece of that power.

Voice is central to power because it's how we advocate, lead, resist, and reimagine. When we speak with intention and clarity, we shift not just conversations but cultures.

Identifying the Silence in Your Own Story

Every woman's silence looks a little different and we often don't recognize it until we start asking questions. Identifying the silence in your own story means looking at where and when your voice went underground. It means noticing the moments you swallowed your truth, staying quiet when something hurt, or hesitating to take up space, not because you lacked something, but because you were taught it was safer to stay small.

This silence might show up in your relationships, your career, your family roles, or even in how you talk to yourself. Maybe it's the apology that's always on your lips. The idea you didn't share in the meeting. The boundary you didn't set. The dream you stopped talking about.

Start by asking:

- Where in my life have I been quiet to stay safe?
- What parts of me did I tone down, hold back, or tuck away to be accepted?
- Whose approval was I trying to earn by not using my voice?

The goal isn't to judge your silence, it's to understand it. Not to blame, but rather to seek clarity. Because once you do, you can begin to choose differently.

My announcement to my family that I wanted to go to college was met with incredulity and a sense that it was a waste of time and money. I went anyway. Looking back, I think this was the beginning of my journey to find my own voice—and use it. It would take many more years and many tough lessons to own it completely.

Before we can reshape the power paradigm, we have to acknowledge that the template for efficacy and power we inherited wasn't built with women in mind. Not just in leadership, but in life. From boardrooms to bedrooms, classrooms to caregiving roles, we've inherited models that expect us to perform rather than belong. To accommodate rather than assert. To carry more while asking for less.

For many of us, finding our voice doesn't happen all at once. It begins quietly, often in the moments when we choose not to betray ourselves. When we say the uncomfortable truth instead of staying silent, when we ask for what we need instead of pretending we're fine, when we finally stop making ourselves smaller to ensure others' comfort.

•

Your voice isn't something you have to earn. You've always had it. The work is simply to dig beneath the layers of expectation, fear, and conditioning to uncover it—and use it.

Finding your voice means tuning in to your essential truth—going back before anyone else's expectations drowned it out. It means standing firmly in the embrace of that truth, even when your hands shake and your voice wavers. And over time, as you choose yourself again and again, your truth-speaking voice grows louder, stronger, and more certain.

We're not after perfection here. We want to show up with honesty and clarity even when it feels hard.

Every time you use your voice, you remind yourself and the world that you matter. That your story is valid. That you don't have to live by a script someone else wrote for you. You don't need a script at all, but if you want one—it should be one you write yourself.

If reclaiming our voice were easy, we'd all be doing it effortlessly. But there are real, powerful forces that make speaking our truth feel risky. The risk of judgment is often the most prevalent. We worry about being seen as difficult, emotional, or "too much." We've internalized the belief that asking for what we need makes us a burden, and that taking up space makes us arrogant.

Perfectionism plays a role, too. It convinces us that, unless we can't speak flawlessly and without hesitation or if there is the slightest chance of getting it "wrong," it's better to stay silent. People-pleasing also keeps us trapped in the cycle of prioritizing others' comfort over our own truth.

On top of that, systemic pressures reinforce these personal fears. In workplaces and social spaces shaped by patriarchal values, women are often penalized for the very qualities that make them powerful—assertiveness, clarity, and emotional honesty.

Every time you choose to speak, even when your voice shakes, you weaken these barriers. And with each moment of courage, your voice grows stronger. I like to call this a quiet rebellion.

The more you use your own voice, the more you create space for others to do the same.

Small, Brave Moments: How to Speak Up

Finding your voice is less about learning how to speak and more about remembering how to listen to yourself. For many of us, the journey begins by noticing just how long we've silenced our own needs, desires, and instincts to meet the expectations of others. Somewhere along the way, we traded our honest voices for the safer roles of peacemaker, performer, or overachiever.

This is not about blame, only awareness. From early childhood, many of us were taught to be "good girls," to stay quiet, be agreeable, and not make waves. We learned which parts of ourselves were acceptable and which were "too much." Over time, we adapted, edited, and performed until our real voices grew faint under the noise of who we thought we were supposed to be.

But here's what I believe. Your voice never left you. It's still there, waiting patiently for you to lower the volume of external expectations and turn inward to listen. The journey to unearthing your voice isn't a straight line, it's a series of small homecomings to yourself. I can attest to this!

As I mentioned earlier, finding your voice doesn't always begin with a bold declaration or a dramatic moment of truth. More often, it starts quietly in small, brave decisions you make every day to live a little more honestly, to show up a little more fully.

- When you say *no* without over-explaining
- When you express your real opinion, even if it feels uncomfortable
- When you ask for what you need, instead of hoping someone will notice you're struggling
- When you share an idea before you've convinced yourself it's perfect

These moments may seem small, but they are acts of courage. Each time you choose to honor your truth; you chip away at the fear that has kept you silent. You begin to trust that your voice matters. Not because it's flawless, but because it's yours.

This is how confidence is built. Not all at once, but through repeated moments of self-trust. And over time, what feels like a whisper grows into a clear, unwavering voice that doesn't shrink for anyone.

Once we find our voices, the next question becomes: how do we help others find theirs? How do we raise a generation of girls who never have to unlearn silence, and boys who understand that true strength lies in listening to and supporting, not silencing, the voices around them?

The work of liberating our voices doesn't end with us. It's a legacy we pass on through how we parent, mentor, and lead. And it begins by changing the conversations we have at home, and modeling the behaviors that honor and support all voices in all areas of our lives.

How to Reinforce These Values Every Day

- **Challenge media messages together:**

  Watch shows and movies with your children and discuss how women and girls are portrayed. Ask critical questions like, "Did the female characters have their own goals?" or "Were they treated as full people or just part of someone else's story?"

- **Model respectful language:**

  Pay attention to the language used at home. Avoid jokes, comments, or phrases that objectify or diminish women and call it out when you hear it. Teach boys that the words they choose and use shape the way they see and treat others. It's important to teach girls this too, as internalized misogyny is very real and often goes unnoticed.

- **Encourage active listening:**

  Teach boys to listen to understand, not just to respond. When girls speak, encourage boys to give them space and time to finish their thoughts without interruption.

- **Talk about consent early and often:**

  Don't save conversations about consent for adulthood. Begin teaching that "no" always means no and that everyone has the right to set boundaries. Starting with everyday situations like sharing toys or respecting personal space.

- **Celebrate empathy and emotional intelligence as strengths:**

  Praise boys for showing kindness, vulnerability, and emotional awareness. Help them see that true strength isn't about dominance, it's about integrity and compassion.

- **Highlight examples of men who advocate for women:**

  Share stories of male leaders who use their power to elevate and support women. Show boys that real leadership means making room for others, not taking up all the space.

Story

My story is not one in particular but a confluence of many and one that I know many of my female peers relate to.

Dating as a woman in your twenties, when you choose the wrong men (like I did), often looks like losing yourself in the hope of being seen. For me, it looked like dating men who needed to be saved, because it felt good to be chosen, even when it meant that I would never choose myself. Being with men that lacked emotional intelligence often ended in me apologizing for even mentioning their hurtful behavior, or their wrong doings. It meant staying silent, and staying complacent in the face of abuse, to make sure I wouldn't hurt their feelings or disturb the peace. It meant putting their emotional needs above my own, hoping the more grace I gave, the more they would respect me. In reality, it's a much lonelier outcome.

Over time, when your feelings and wants are ignored, the "I'll change, I'm sorry"'s become empty promises and repeating patterns, you begin to stop asking. I went unheard for so long, that I stopped speaking. They used anger and detachment as tools, making me question my reality, my worth, and my right to have a voice in my own life. For too long, I mistook their emotional immaturity for depth, when in truth, it was manipulation.

Chapter 3:

The Voice Within

"The truth will set you free. But first it will piss you off."
– Gloria Steinem

Before we can raise our voices in the world, it's important to hear it within ourselves first. So many of us move through life performing versions of ourselves that feel acceptable, competent, or safe, but far from authentic. Reconnecting with your voice doesn't begin with speaking out. It begins with tuning in.

This chapter is about the quiet, often uncomfortable, work of listening to what's true inside us. The voice we've been taught to ignore, minimize, or override. The one that whispers what we really want. What we really believe. What we've known all along.

I'll never forget the time my godparents came to California to visit after I had been living there for a number of years. My brothers and I spent a lot of time with them growing up after our father died. My godmother was my aunt--my father's sister.

Growing up, my godparents often told me that being a girl meant I didn't need help with homework because I didn't need to worry about school. The implication being that I would get married and have babies, so school wasn't as important as it was for my brothers. When they bought a little go cart for my brothers, I wasn't allowed to ride in it because I was a girl. They took my brothers on trips and left me behind. When they took my brothers bowling, I was given a few dollars instead because bowling wasn't for little girls. I always knew that this wasn't right, and my inner voice gnawed at me. At times I resented my godparents.

Fast forward to California. I was in my early 20s and had come to the state fresh out of college, not knowing anyone, to start my life away from the confines of my family and the small township where I grew up. My godparents took me and my then-boyfriend to dinner. Guess what? They apologized! They said that all of those ideas and misconceptions were simply the way they were raised and they, unjustly, imposed those beliefs on me. Ha! Vindication!

Of course, in many ways, the damage had been done, but this apology was another turning point for me. While some might consider my move to California fearless, I still didn't trust my own voice.

Reconnecting with Your Truth

Truth isn't always loud. In fact, it often makes itself known first in a quiet whisper. The pit in your stomach when something's off, the tug in your chest when you know you're ready for more. But in a world that conditions women to second-guess, self-edit, and perform, those signals can be easy to dismiss. The patriarchy depends on us ignoring our voices and relinquishing our agency. Like it or not, we are still swimming in male waters and must learn how to navigate the waves, so we don't drown. So, we self-edit, second-guess, and perform. The current power structure depends on it.

We may say, "I don't know what I want," when the truth is we've been taught it's safer not to want. Or we mistake someone else's wants as our own. We may say, "I'm fine," when we've been conditioned to believe that discomfort is something to swallow, not name. Or we may not even be able to identify the discomfort. We often say, "This is fine," when the limitations are, in fact, intolerable. And because we are conditioned to care for the needs of others as a way to find validation, we often can't identify our own needs.

Reconnecting with your voice means getting quiet enough to hear yourself think. It means asking, not what does everyone else need from me, but what do *I* need, believe, crave, or desire?

For a very long time, I had no idea what I wanted or needed. I certainly couldn't identify my inner emotions. My voice was stifled and dismissed for as long as I can remember. My voice was not my own. At times I still feel my voice being dismissed by family, friends, and colleagues.

Finding the connection to myself took some doing. There was even a time when I wasn't sure I knew what being happy meant or felt like. I was out of touch and confused. It took moving three thousand miles away from my family and everything I thought I knew to even begin to figure it all out.

As a young girl around eight or nine and even in my teenage years, I remember spending a great deal of time alone in my room listening to music and struggling to untangle my feelings and thoughts about my life and the world around me. I was able to express some of my emotions through the music I listened to in the privacy and safety of my room. Many of you reading this book probably relate to this scenario. The songs spanned my emotions and my consciousness from Simon and Garfunkel's "I Am a Rock," "Sounds of Silence," and "Bridge over Troubled Waters" to Helen Reddy's "I Am Woman" and Bob Dylan's "Blowin' in the Wind." To name a few.

This process isn't always linear. At first, it can feel like untangling a knot you didn't know was there. You may uncover buried disappointments, unspoken dreams, or truths about yourself and your ideas that you didn't realize you had silenced. You may find grief where you expected clarity, or anger where you expected confidence. That's okay. These emotions are signs you're getting closer to something real.

Reconnecting with your truth also means giving yourself permission to evolve. The version of truth you held ten, twenty, or forty years ago may no longer serve the woman you're becoming. You're allowed to update your beliefs, your desires, and your definition of what's possible. I am most definitely not the woman I was 10 or 20 years ago. And I'll continue to evolve, I hope.

Sometimes reconnecting with our truth shakes things up. Relationships shift. Jobs become untenable. Old dreams start to crumble so new ones can rise. But clarity, even when it disrupts, is a path home.

I've lost friends over the years. Some due to my evolution, some due to theirs. It wasn't always easy, but in each case, both parties are probably the better for it.

Self-Trust and Emotional Honesty

We can't use our voices if we don't trust them. And we can't feel that trust if we're constantly overriding our emotional truths.

Self-trust is built moment by moment. It's built when you feel anger and name it, instead of explaining it away. It's built when you feel joy and let yourself fully experience it, instead of downplaying it. It's built when you listen to your inner knowing even if it goes against the grain.

Many of us were taught that emotions are dangerous, especially the "loud" ones. Anger. Desire. Disappointment. But emotional honesty isn't a weakness. It's wisdom. Emotions are information. They tell us when something matters, where a boundary is needed, if it is time for change.

The voice within becomes clearer when we stop policing our feelings and honor them instead.

When we choose to meet our emotions with honesty and without judgment, we slowly dismantle the internalized belief that our feelings are liabilities. We begin to understand them as signals, guiding us toward what we need to pay attention to. Self-trust deepens when we listen to those signals and respond with care rather than suppression.

Reclaiming our voices begins with reclaiming our emotional truths. Not every emotion requires action, but every emotion deserves acknowledgement. And the more we trust ourselves to hold space for what we feel, the more we trust ourselves to speak from a place of truth.

Intuition and Values as Our Guide

In a noisy world, how do we know what's real?

Our intuition, our internal guidance system, is often drowned out by the volume of external expectations. While intuition seems mysterious, it's more like a muscle. And like any muscle, it strengthens with use. The more we listen to it, the stronger the connection and the easier it becomes to hear it.

When we begin to recognize the patterns of what feels right vs. what feels performative, what energizes vs. what depletes, we develop a deeper attunement to ourselves. Intuition is not about certainty, it's about alignment. It asks, "Does this feel true?" rather than "Will this be approved?"

Pairing intuition with clearly defined values. What matters most to you, what you're willing and unwilling to compromise, gives you an internal compass no system can take away. Your values become the boundaries that protect your voice. Your intuition becomes the path back to it.

When values are rooted, your voice becomes harder to silence. When intuition is honored, your direction becomes clearer, even when the path is uncertain.

In the lives of many women, this alignment with intuition and values often becomes visible in quiet but radical choices: walking away from relationships that no longer serve us, that harm us and silence us, or leaving careers that stifle joy or devalue our contributions or speaking truths that shift harmful family legacies and heal trauma. These acts are not always celebrated, but they are deeply powerful.

We live in a world that often trains us to defer to external authority. But true authority begins within. When you know what matters to you and you trust your sense of what feels right, you become a leader in your own life—not a follower of rules you did not create or approve of and that don't serve you.

Finding Clarity, Even When It Shakes Things Up

Clarity is powerful. But it isn't always convenient.

Sometimes clarity arrives like a lightning bolt: a sudden knowing that something has to change. Other times, it comes slowly, through quiet reflection or years of discomfort we can no longer justify. One day, you see the tiny flower of clarity pushing through the cracks in the wall of silence built by others.

Regardless of how it arrives, clarity disrupts. It invites hard conversations, big decisions, and honest reassessments. It may push us into transition or demand we reconfigure what we thought our lives would look like. But clarity is a gift even when it breaks things open.

Because in that rupture, something new becomes possible. Something more aligned, more rooted, more alive.

To live unmuted is not just to speak, it's to live in alignment with your deepest truth. And that truth, no matter how long it's been buried, is still there. Waiting. Ready. Whole.

That voice within is not lost. It's recalling, recognizing, and reminding us. And when we listen, really listen, it starts to grow.

Story

At 21, I was the youngest Account Manager at a Fortune 500 company, and the only person of color on a team of over 25. I had worked incredibly hard to earn my seat at the table, but looking back, I realize part of what allowed me to rise quickly wasn't just my dedication. It was also my silence.

I stayed quiet when leaders made jokes about my race. I stayed quiet when my own manager commented on my appearance or said things like, "You don't even look Black." I stayed quiet the day after the Nike-Kaepernick controversy, when she came up to my desk and said, "Well, I guess I'm not buying Nike anymore." Those moments never felt good, but I feared that if I spoke up, they'd find a way to label me as "the crazy, young, Black, too-woke liberal" and push me out. So I kept my head down.

Then, in 2020, after George Floyd's murder, my company held an open DEI forum. For the first time, I shared my truth. In front of our CEO, VP of People, my HR representative, and colleagues, I told them what I had experienced over the past four years under this same manager, who was still at the company. They were horrified.

But instead of holding her accountable or creating a safe space for me, they told me the best way forward was to schedule a Zoom call with her, to personally explain why her comments were harmful. After years of silence born from fear of retaliation, I was being asked to confront the very person who had silenced me, and to take on the role of her DEI educator. I told them I didn't want to bear that burden, especially as the only Black woman on the team, but they insisted this was the only solution.

In the end, I realized I had been silenced twice: once by fear, and once by leadership deciding how, when, and if my voice was allowed to be heard.

Chapter 4:

Courage in Action - Speaking Up, Even When It's Hard

"We cannot accept any code or creed that uniformly defrauds woman of all her natural rights"
— Elizabeth Cady Stanton

We often associate courage with physical risk taking, public protests, whistleblowing, or standing alone in a boardroom. But courage isn't necessarily dramatic, public, or grand. Courage happens in the smallest, most personal moments. It shows up in the decision to tell the truth when staying silent would be easier. It lives in the space between knowing what you feel and daring to say it out loud. Courage is not courage without fear, or at least trepidation, to be overcome. This includes fear of failure, rejection, retaliation, or isolation.

I want to talk about those moments. The ones where we're asked to choose between comfort and authenticity. It's about what it means to speak up, not just when it's safe, but when it matters— and is hard. For women, this takes on an added layer of courage. Because no matter when and where we choose to speak up or speak out, we face the double bind of navigating the world while female.

Over time, authenticity becomes less and less uncomfortable until, one day, you realize that being silent and inauthentic is now what feels all wrong.

Courage in Everyday Life

Courage isn't always bold or loud. Sometimes, it can be admitting to your friend you're hurt. Sometimes, it means finally saying no to a request you can't fulfill. Other times, it means putting your name on an idea you believe in, even if it might be rejected. Sometimes it's joining a public protest or donating to a cause you believe in.

For women, courage often comes at a cost. When we speak up, we risk being labeled difficult, dramatic, or emotional. We are tasked with being clearer in our communications with men only to be told we are a bitch or aggressive when we are. So, we lower our voices and calm our words only to be told to sit down, we don't have the temperament to play with the 'big boys,' or we're too emotional if we get frustrated.

We've been conditioned to prioritize harmony over honesty, to be likable rather than disruptive. But every time we choose truth over comfort, our voices grow stronger. And the more we do it, the less terrifying it becomes.

I know many people, men and women alike, who don't find my boldness likeable. I've made peace with that. I am comfortable in my boldness.

Because courage is not the absence of fear, it means moving forward with your truth despite that fear. It doesn't always feel good in the moment. But it builds something important: inner alignment. A sense of living in integrity with who you are.

I'm not saying it's easy or that I get it right all of the time. Quite the contrary. Sure, I temper it when necessary and sometimes even stay silent (though those who know me will tell you that isn't often). But I know my values—and my value—and I never stay silent when those are challenged.

Back in the 70s, I was a teenager when I walked to ratify the Equal Rights Amendment (ERA). It was a 5k walk where you obtained sponsorship donations for each mile. My stepfather refused to sponsor me. He was certain that if the ERA passed it would mean that anyone could watch pornography on TV and men and women would have to use the same public bathrooms. I find it interesting that a similar argument is being made now regarding trans people and bathrooms and boy would he be freaking out about how easy it is to find pornography on the internet now! It made no sense to me at the time, but it did to him. My mother also refused to sponsor me when asked in front of my stepfather. When she drove me to the meeting site for the walk, she privately told me that she would sponsor me but not to tell my stepfather. Being the righteous, rebellious teenager I was, I told her I didn't want her sponsorship if she couldn't support me out loud.

Over the years, I've looked back at that moment, I realize what I could not see then. She was using her voice in the only way she felt safe to do so. She wasn't afraid of physical violence, she was afraid of using her voice, a voice that sounded different than her husband's. She was afraid of very real consequences in her marriage if she did—with 5 children and no way to make a living on her own, the consequences could have been dire. Though I doubt they would have divorced, it may not have been a risk she was willing to take. She was most definitely a product of her era, culture, and environment. And her supporting me in private was the most courageous thing she could do. I wish I had been able to see that then.

Boundaries, Boldness, and Emotional Resilience

Speaking up often means setting a boundary. It means saying, "This is what I need," or "That doesn't work for me," even when those words feel risky. Boundaries are not walls. They're bridges to healthier relationships. They create clarity, safety, and space for mutual respect. When others are upset by our boundaries, that's a red flag.

I get questioned about this often in my coaching practice. I'm asked questions like "How can I set a boundary without being rude or hurting someone else?" "What's a boundary look like?"

or "What do I do if someone doesn't respect a boundary I set?" I get asked these questions by men and women alike.

Boundaries are one of the most powerful forms of self-expression and yet for many women, they're also the most difficult. They require us to name our limits, assert our needs, and risk disappointing others. In a world that has taught women to be agreeable, accommodating, and self-sacrificing, boundaries can feel like betrayal, or even aggression.

We are often praised for our flexibility, our willingness to say yes, our emotional labor, our ability to "just make it work." But the flip side of that praise is burnout, resentment, and disconnection from our own needs. Somewhere along the way, many of us internalized the message that setting a boundary is mean, selfish, or too "aggressive." But what are these words code for? When women are called "mean" it usually just indicates they are acting in a way that is inconvenient for the other person. And selfish? Looking out for ourselves is demonized as selfish, when it certainly is not considered selfish in a man. Aggressive is the insult used against women who are assertive—an "unfeminine" quality. Women have been programmed to believe that protecting our energy is less important than keeping the peace.

One reason boundaries feel so hard is that many of us were never taught what they actually are. A boundary isn't a punishment or a wall. Contrary to what I hear from both men and women, it's not about pushing people away, it's about protecting what matters most: our well-being, our values, our integrity, and our time. Boundaries are the lines that define where we end and someone else begins. They are the voice that says, *This is okay with me. This is not.*

But when we've been conditioned to confuse our worth with selflessness, even recognizing those lines can feel foreign. Some people fear setting boundaries because they associate it with conflict or rejection. Others have been in environments where their boundaries were consistently violated, ignored, questioned, or punished so they learned to stay silent to stay safe. And in systems that prize productivity over humanity, many have been rewarded for over-functioning while being penalized for protecting their limits.

The truth is that unspoken boundaries don't keep us safe, they keep us stuck. And unclear boundaries don't avoid conflict, they invite confusion, burnout, and erosion of trust.

Understanding boundaries begins with understanding ourselves: What do I need to feel safe, valued, respected? Where am I saying yes when I mean no? Where have I mistaken self-abandonment for kindness?

Admittedly, I'm still not completely clear on my own boundaries, without realizing it in the moment. It's only later that I see where I could have and should have set a boundary or been clearer with others about my boundaries. Thankfully, over the years, I get it right more and more.

Reclaiming our voice means learning to say, "This is enough," "This matters to me," or "Not right now" without apology. By reclaiming our voice in this way, we can begin to change the paradigm.

Setting boundaries is honest and respectful. We're teaching others how to be in relationship with us. And we're modeling for other women, and for the next generation, that taking up space includes taking care of ourselves.

Reclaiming Time, Energy and Emotional Labor: Saying Yes to What Matters Most

Time is one of our most precious resources and one of the first things we give away when we feel we have to prove our worth. For many women, our time is constantly fragmented: meetings that run over, errands that fall to us by default, text messages we answer immediately even when we're exhausted, favors we say yes to before we even check in with ourselves.

In my experience, this isn't just a scheduling issue. It's a cultural issue. I am much more protective of my time than I was when I was younger. It's partly a function of getting older—I have less time to play around with—but it's also a product of the painstaking work I've done on myself over the years. Once again, not perfect, but a work in progress.

Women are socialized to equate value with availability. We're taught to feel guilty for resting, selfish for prioritizing our needs, and irresponsible for saying no. But when our calendars are filled with obligations that don't reflect our values, we don't just lose time, we lose ourselves.

Reclaiming your time doesn't mean being rigid. It's about being intentional. It's the act of looking at your days and asking: *What am I building with this time? Who am I giving it to? And does this reflect what I truly want my life to stand for?*

Saying no or setting this boundary is not a rejection of others, it's an affirmation of your priorities. And protecting your time is how you make space for the work, rest, relationships, and creative energy that fuel your voice. It's an action that says, "*I matter.*"

It's possible to say yes with your mouth while your body says no.

Chronic fatigue, burnout, anxiety, restlessness—these health concerns are often symptoms of over-extension. Of giving more than we have, more than we can sustainably offer, more than we even realize until something breaks.

Many women are masters of pushing through. We can show up, smile, deliver, and exceed expectations, all while running on fumes. We are often expected to do twice as much in half the time or as the saying goes "backwards and in heels." And because the world often rewards us for this level of performance, we rarely pause long enough to ask: *At what cost?*

Energy is not just physical. It's emotional, creative, and relational. Every conversation, task, and decision pulls from that reservoir. Reclaiming energy means identifying the hidden drains: the one-sided friendships, the unspoken obligations, the perfectionism that fuels the lack of self-worth.

It means recognizing that "doing it all" is not the goal. Being well enough to do what matters most *is*. But we've been sold the lie that we could and should strive to have it all. The problem is the only way we could have it all is by *doing* it all. Unlike our male counterparts who can have it all by doing the bare minimum! And this is an impossible task. I think we need to redefine what 'having it all' really means to each of us as an individual.

When we reclaim our energy, we stop measuring success by how much we've endured. We begin to define it by how much we've aligned with our values, our joy, and our own well-being.

Emotional labor is the unpaid, often unnoticed effort of managing emotions, your own and everyone else's. It's smoothing over conflict, remembering birthdays, interpreting moods, absorbing tension, and constantly monitoring the emotional temperature of a room.

It's something women are expected to do without acknowledgement, let alone compensation. Often, men do not even realize that emotional labor exists because they are so used to women simply doing it all.

In families, women are often the default emotional caretakers. In the workplace, we're expected to be empathetic but not emotional, supportive but not demanding, flexible but still flawless. We are the mediators, the listeners, the morale-boosters, the calm in the storm even when we're falling apart inside.

Reclaiming your voice includes naming this labor. It includes saying, "I'm carrying too much," or "This isn't mine to hold." It's asking for shared responsibility. It's refusing to equate emotional invisibility with strength. This was one of the most powerful lessons for me to learn. It changed my life.

Making emotional labor visible means honoring it as *real work*. And it means refusing to make peace with systems, relationships, or roles that depend on your silence to stay comfortable.

I think boldness is often misunderstood. It's not about aggression or dominance. It's about clarity and self-respect. Boldness is applying for the job you think you're only 70% qualified for. It's sharing your opinion in a room full of louder voices. It's deciding to take up space on the page, in a meeting, in your own life.

When I was career coaching, I worked with men and women. The men would apply for jobs that they were maybe 50% qualified and feel confident about it! Many of the women would tell me that they couldn't apply for a particular job because they didn't have 100% of the qualifications.

These were the same women who had no idea that they could negotiate their salary when offered a position. Men negotiated. In fact, it was generally expected of them.

In my current practice with entrepreneurial women, I find, more often than not, they are either giving away services and expertise or not charging nearly enough. This could be a reflection of many things including lack of self-worth and imposter syndrome but a fear of being too bold seems to play a part.

Emotional resilience is what allows us to speak up again after being dismissed. It's what helps us recover after a tough conversation, regroup after criticism, and keep showing up with our full selves.

Resilience doesn't mean you never feel shaken. It means you don't stay stuck. It's the quiet power that carries you through vulnerability and into courage again. For women, emotional resilience is often forged in the unseen places, navigating work while managing caregiving, grieving in private while performing in public, staying composed in rooms where your presence is questioned.

It means having the capacity to return to your voice, again and again, even when the world tells you it's too much, too loud, too inconvenient. Resilience allows us to repair, not just relationships or reputations, but our own belief in the power of our voices. It says, *"Yes, that was hard. And yes, I'm still here."*

In a world that often demands perfection, emotional resilience is a radical form of power and protest. It reminds us that we can be imperfect and still be worthy. That we can falter and still be strong. That we can speak up, get it wrong, and still return to the table.

Reclaiming time, energy, and emotional labor might sound small but they are radical acts of agency. Each one is a way of saying: *I matter. My needs matter. My voice matters.*

These aren't selfish acts. They are how we sustain our strength. How we stop performing invincibility and start building a life rooted in truth, integrity, and wholeness.

They are how we live unmuted.

Navigating Fear, Conflict, and Risk

Let's be honest: speaking up is not always met with applause. I can attest to that! Sometimes it brings tension, conflict, or unwanted consequences. That's why so many women choose silence. Not because they lack something to say, but because they've been punished for saying it before.

Navigating these moments takes awareness. Not every space is safe. Not every audience is ready to hear what you have to say. But even when we choose silence to protect ourselves, we can still hold our truth internally. The goal isn't to speak in a reckless manner, something I've gotten better at over the years but still struggle with! The goal is to stay connected to your truth and share it where and when it matters most.

Fear doesn't go away. But it doesn't have to run the show. You can feel afraid and still speak. You can fear rejection and still raise your hand. The point isn't to eliminate risk. It's to remind yourself that your voice is worth the risk. Our voices are worth the risk.

Conflict and unmuting can feel terrifying, especially if you've been taught that harmony is the highest virtue. At first, unmuting can be scary and difficult, but it ultimately leads us to a kind of authentic serenity. Sometimes, conflict is where change begins. Speaking up might shake things up but shaking things up can be the first step toward realignment. Disruption isn't the enemy of peace; silence in the face of injustice is.

Speaking Up, Even When the World Pushes Back

Throughout history, women have stepped into conflict not because it was safe but because staying silent was no longer an option. Their courage wasn't born from comfort. It was born from urgency. From knowing that real change only comes when someone dares to challenge the status quo created by generations of those in power. Let's not forget that we were never 'given' the right to vote, we fought for it.

In the early 20th century, the women's suffrage movement in the U.S. and abroad was met with brutal resistance. Women like Alice Paul, Sojourner Truth, Emmeline Pankhurst, and countless unnamed activists faced arrest, violence, and social ostracization for demanding something as basic as the right to vote. They were jailed, put in mental hospitals, and went on hunger strikes. They were dismissed as irrational, dangerous, disruptive. Nevertheless, they persisted. Their voices cracked open a door that had been shut for centuries.

In the 1960s and '70s, the feminist movement grew into a broader wave of social and political activism. Leaders like Gloria Steinem, Angela Davis, and Betty Friedan used their platforms not just to advocate for women's rights, but to center issues of race, class, and sexuality in conversations about power and justice. Speaking up meant risking reputations, careers, and even personal safety. But these women redefined what leadership could look like from the streets to the Senate.

More recently, the *#MeToo* movement became a cultural reckoning. What started as a grassroots campaign by Tarana Burke to support survivors of sexual violence turned into a global conversation on abuse, silence, and systemic complicity. When survivors came forward often at great personal and professional risk, they exposed not only individual harm, but cultural patterns that had gone unchallenged for generations.

And then there are the lesser-known changemakers like Marsha P. Johnson, a self-identified Black drag queen and transgender activist who was a key figure in the early LGBTQ+ rights movement and the Stonewall uprising. Though often erased from mainstream histories, Johnson's voice, protest, and relentless advocacy for trans women and unhoused queer youth in New York City helped lay the foundation for the very concept of intersectional justice.

Today, Gen Z women are picking up the mic not just digitally, but globally. Young women are using their voices with striking clarity, urgency, and reach. They've grown up in a world on fire literally and metaphorically and they aren't waiting for permission to lead.

Take Zyahna Bryant, a community organizer who, at just 15 years old, launched a petition to remove a Confederate statue in Charlottesville, Virginia. Or Amika George, a British-Indian activist who founded the *#FreePeriods* campaign to end period poverty in the U.K. before she was even out of high school. And Greta Thunberg, recognized for her environmental activism, also exemplifies the courage it takes to speak truth to power when the stakes are global, and the resistance is fierce.

These Gen Z leaders are fluent in intersectionality. They understand that gender equity cannot be separated from racial justice, economic access, climate resilience, and mental health. They are not waiting for institutions to change, they are demanding it, designing it, and documenting it, often in real time on social media platforms that make their voices harder to ignore and causing a great deal of discomfort for many men.

Social media has become the latest front line for courageous speech. A single post or video can spark global movements, forcing the world to confront injustice it would rather look away from. It has unleashed voices once contained to kitchen tables or whispered to friends, connecting them across continents in solidarity. Survivors of assault, victims of racial violence, and communities denied visibility have used these platforms to amplify truth in real time, creating digital reckonings that cannot be ignored.

But the same platforms that amplify truth also invite backlash. Women, people of color, queer voices, and anyone who dares to expose injustice are met with harassment, ridicule, and attempts to silence them. The paradox of social media is that it is both microphone and target, lifeline and battlefield. Yet the courage to keep posting, to keep sharing, to keep raising voices in the face of digital hostility is itself a radical act of unmuting. These women are not waiting for permission or for power to grant them space; they are taking it, one post at a time.

Today, women in the U.S. are once again at the frontlines, this time fighting to reclaim bodily autonomy in the wake of the Supreme Court's 2022 decision to overturn *Roe v. Wade*. Across the country, women are speaking out against state-level restrictions on reproductive care, criminalization of miscarriage, and legislation that prioritizes control over compassion. From grassroots organizers in red states to healthcare workers risking arrest to provide care, the battle for autonomy is not theoretical—it is immediate, personal, and deeply political. And they are meeting the moment with creativity, collaboration, and clarity.

These moments, movements, and leaders remind us that speaking up is rarely easy, but it is always necessary. And whether you're raising your voice in a courtroom, a boardroom, a classroom, or a kitchen table, you're part of a lineage that stretches across generations. A lineage of women who said the thing that wasn't supposed to be said, who asked the questions that disrupted the room, who named what others were too afraid to acknowledge.

Courageous speech is not just about volume. It's about vision. And the women of Gen Z are making it clear: the future will not be muted.

Each of these movements and moments show us that conflict is not something to avoid. Rather, conflict is often where the cracks in a broken system let the light in. And while not all of us will lead national or global movements, we each have the ability to say the things that need to be said, to name what others avoid, and to change the story, one voice at a time.

There will be times when your voice is met with resistance, defensiveness, or dismissal. That doesn't mean you were wrong to speak. It means your truth challenged the comfort of the room. Sometimes, that's exactly what needs to happen.

Courageous speech requires preparation and support. It's okay to rehearse. It's okay to seek backup. It's okay to choose your moment. Power doesn't come from being reckless. It comes from being intentional, steady, and clear. And it grows every time you choose to honor your truth, no matter the outcome.

Conflict, Courage, and the Cost of Silence

Conflict is often portrayed as something to be avoided. The message is clear: conflict is messy, emotional, disruptive. For many women, conflict has long been synonymous with danger. Not just in the physical sense, but in the psychological and professional realms too. We've been socialized to be fearful of conflict because we've been penalized for engaging in it.

Ask a woman who challenged a male colleague in a meeting and was labeled "difficult" or was laid off a month later. Ask the mother who advocated fiercely for her child's needs and was called "pushy." Ask the woman who set a boundary in a relationship and was dismissed as "too emotional." Conflict doesn't always mean yelling or aggression, it can be as subtle as tension in a conversation, the withdrawal of support, or the slow erosion of opportunity. Women who speak up are often sidelined, their jobs "eliminated," and their career paths blocked.

But courageous speech means being willing to engage thoughtfully, intentionally, and with the discomfort that conflict brings. It doesn't mean going to battle every time you perceive injustice, but it does mean refusing to make yourself small to keep the peace.

Courageous speech today is about naming the dynamics others avoid. It's speaking up about the double standards at work, the microaggressions in the meeting, the imbalance in the home. It's saying the thing that's been left unsaid, not to provoke, but to shift the paradigm.

And let's be clear: this takes more than confidence. It takes context. Many women must navigate layers of bias based on race, class, age, ability, and more. The risk of speaking up is not the same for everyone. So courageous speech must also be supported speech. It must be met with policies that protect allies who stand beside those speaking up, and cultures that learn to listen rather than retaliate.

There is courage in refusing to perform politeness when harm is being done. In saying "no" clearly and without apology. In disrupting systems that depend on our silence. By doing so, we move the needle. Having a career should not require constant acts of courage.

Courageous conflict isn't about creating chaos. It's about restoring alignment between what we believe and what we're willing to allow. It's how we reclaim voice, not just as individuals, but as a collective force for change.

The Power of Naming What Others Avoid

There's a particular kind of power in saying the thing everyone else is tiptoeing around. When we name the truth in the room—

the dynamic, the imbalance, and the harm—we can shift a conversation, a system, even a culture.

I'm not talking about being provocative for its own sake. What matters is being clear, honest, and courageous in the face of denial or avoidance. When women name what others avoid—the inequity, exclusion and unfairness—we disrupt the comfort of silence. We hold up a mirror to what's been normalized and say, "We can do better."

Naming what others avoid doesn't require a microphone or a podium. Sometimes, it's a question asked in a meeting: "Whose voices are missing here?" Sometimes, it's saying, "That joke wasn't funny." Sometimes, it's offering an alternative perspective when a group is too eager to move forward without reflection.

This kind of truth-telling takes discernment and inner steadiness. It requires being able to sit with discomfort, yours and others'. And it's rarely met with instant gratitude. But over time, it creates a culture where truth has room to breathe, and allows people to learn to listen, reflect, and change.

Like intuition, naming what others avoid is a muscle. The more you use it, the stronger it gets. And each time you do, you model what's possible. You give others permission to speak more honestly, to engage more deeply, and to show up more fully.

Let's not trade truth for ease. Your voice is a disruptive, necessary force. Use it, even when it shakes the room. Especially then.

Because your voice is not just yours. It's a spark. And when you use it, it lights the way for others.

ORE · NO MORE · NO MORE

EN · STOLEN · STOLE

ERS · SISTE

Story

At 27, my life changed overnight. I unexpectedly became the guardian of my six year old niece, a little girl who had already endured years of trauma and was living with ADHD. At first, I thought it would be temporary, so I only asked my company for a few days of flexibility. But as weeks turned into months, it became clear: I wasn't just helping out, I was becoming her permanent parent.

That year was the hardest of my life. My niece was having emotional outbursts both at home and at school. She was getting sick almost every other week. My days were full of school meetings, doctor visits, and therapy appointments, all while trying to create a safe and stable home for her. My career, something I had always poured myself into, inevitably took a back seat. I was still meeting my goals, but I wasn't surpassing them the way my manager had come to expect from me.

When promotion season came around, I was told I wouldn't be moving forward. The reason? My manager said she was worried I wasn't "ready" because of everything going on in my personal life. I pushed back, reminding her that I had consistently excelled for three years and that the past six months of needing flexibility shouldn't erase my accomplishments. Her response cut deep: "There are other moms in our organization who seem to excel in this role just fine. Maybe you can get some tips from them."

In that moment, I felt completely invisible. My reality, being a young, single woman suddenly raising a traumatized child, was dismissed and minimized. I wasn't seen for the resilience it took to show up every day and still meet expectations. Instead, I was compared to women whose journeys looked nothing like mine, women who had partners at home, planned their families, and had maternity leave to prepare. My voice and my truth didn't seem to matter.

Chapter 5:

Unlearning & Rewriting the Rules

"If they don't give you a seat at the table, bring a folding chair"
— Shirley Chisholm

W hat holds us back is learned: roles we've absorbed, conventions and directives we've internalized, labels we've been handed. Many of us have moved through life burdened by silent rules we never agreed to. Rules that instructed us to be pleasing, perfect, accommodating, modest. That told us ambition was selfish, confidence was arrogance, and power had to look like control.

This chapter is an invitation to unlearn all that.

Let's dismantle the belief systems that no longer serve us. In fact, they never served us. They served a system inside which we needed to survive. Now we can let go of the masks, the performances, the roles that were assigned instead of chosen. Let's build a version of power that is grounded in voice, value, and authenticity.

Perfectionism: The Illusion of Worth as Flawlessness

Perfectionism—and perfection—is often praised in our culture, especially in women. It looks like high achievement, drive, and discipline. But under the surface, perfectionism is a strategy, a way to avoid judgment, shame, or failure. It's not about healthy striving; it's about fear. Fear of not being enough. Fear of disappointing others. Fear of what might happen if we show up as we really are.

The idea of honoring men's growth as people and as professionals, which naturally includes learning, risking, failing, and then succeeding, often feels like an unspoken free pass. Men are permitted to stumble and still be seen as capable. Women, on the other hand, are held to expectations of flawlessness. That difference is one of the clearest signals that we are not allowed the same leeway.

When a woman steps into a male-dominated field, she does not get the same grace to learn and adapt. If she is not immediately successful, makes a mistake, or needs to relearn and try again, the response is too often dismissive: "See, she does not belong here." No one says that when a man falters. He is given the benefit of the doubt. She is given the burden of proof.

This is not simply a double standard. It is a gatekeeping mechanism that keeps women on trial while men are allowed to evolve. He is allowed to fail forward. She is expected to arrive perfected.

For many women, perfectionism begins early. We learn that being "good" means being quiet, tidy, agreeable, and impressive. It's reinforced every time we are rewarded for getting it right the first time or punished, directly or indirectly, for asking too much, crying too loud, or wanting our needs met rather than ignored or silenced. We internalize the idea that approval comes when we perform. That love is earned through achievement or body perfection set by societal standards. That mistakes or anything outside of the standard means we are flawed.

But perfectionism doesn't protect us. It isolates us. It keeps us stuck in self-doubt, procrastination, and burnout. And it convinces us that our value is conditional, that we must constantly prove we are enough.

Releasing perfectionism doesn't mean lowering your standards—only now they are your standards instead of someone else's. It means redefining success in terms of authenticity, growth, and joy. It means making space for mistakes and humanity. It means understanding that wholeness matters more than polish.

Award-winning actor, Jamie Lee Curtis, has openly shared her journey of overcoming the pressures of perfectionism and societal expectations. A critical comment about her appearance led her to undergo cosmetic surgery, which initiated a long struggle with addiction. Eventually, she emerged as a strong advocate for self-acceptance and redefining beauty standards, encouraging others to embrace their natural selves without shame or pressure.

Ashley Graham, a prominent plus-size model, has been a proponent of body positivity and the Health at Every Size movement. In 2016, she became the first size 16 model to be featured on the cover of Sports Illustrated Swimsuit Issue. Graham has used her platform to advocate for self-acceptance and challenge traditional beauty standards.

When Perfection Becomes Performance

Perfectionism isn't just about what shows up in the mirror. Sometimes, it shows up in our calendars, our inboxes, our to-do lists. It's the kind of perfectionism that tells us we can never slow down, never mess up, never disappoint. It hides behind phrases like "I've got it" and "no problem," even when we're overwhelmed, under-resourced, and running on empty.

For many women, achievement becomes armor. We over-deliver not because we want to impress, but because we're afraid of what will happen if we don't. We fear being seen as unreliable, unworthy, or incapable, so we keep striving. Not out of inspiration, but out of fear.

This kind of perfectionism is reinforced early, too. Girls are praised for being "responsible," "organized," "hard-working." But rarely are they praised for resting. Rarely are they taught that doing "enough" is actually enough. We don't teach girls to pace themselves. We teach them to prove themselves.

Brené Brown calls this the hustle for worthiness. And it's exhausting.

Author and activist Reshma Saujani, founder of *Girls Who Code*, talks openly about her journey through this kind of perfectionism. She began her career following what she called the "perfect immigrant daughter script": top grades, an Ivy League education, and a career in law. But despite checking every box, she felt disconnected from her purpose. After an unsuccessful run for Congress, she pivoted, letting go of the high-achieving, risk-averse identity she had been raised to uphold. She went on to found *Girls Who Code*, an organization that has empowered hundreds of thousands of girls to pursue careers in tech.

In her book *Brave, Not Perfect*, Saujani challenges the notion that success comes from doing everything "right." Instead, she advocates for courage over compliance and authenticity over approval. Her journey is a powerful reminder that stepping out of a role that looks successful from the outside can be the first step toward real impact.

Her breakthrough came not from doing more, but from doing differently, letting go of "perfect" in order to lead with courage and authenticity.

When perfectionism is tied to performance, it convinces us that rest is weakness and vulnerability is failure. But real power doesn't come from proving. It comes from choosing what matters, what's sustainable, and what's true for us.

Unlearning this version of perfectionism is messy. It requires dropping the mask. It may even feel like failure. But freedom waits on the other side—the freedom to succeed on your own terms, not someone else's scorecard.

There are a number of underlying factors that contribute to perfectionism. Fear, shame, the need for control, and societal pressure to name a few. Perfectionism is the unwillingness to accept anything that isn't perfect. This might seem like a good thing because it provides us with a level of approval and what feels like success. But it keeps us in black and white thinking which, in turn, can keep us paralyzed from making any decisions. Perfection is impossible to attain; therefore, we can never achieve the feeling of being enough. Anorexia is perfectionism that kills as young women (mostly) strive for control and/or acceptance.

People-Pleasing: The Habit That Silences Us

People-pleasing, too, is often rooted in survival. We learn to attune to others, to anticipate needs, to smooth the edges in a room. We become hyper-aware of how we're being perceived and what everyone else is feeling, which becomes our responsibility too. That awareness keeps us from asking for what we need. We neglect ourselves. People-pleasers have a strong desire for approval, validation, and social acceptance from others. Setting boundaries is difficult. At its worst, people-pleasing can be harmful when it leads to emotional depletion, resentment, and a lack of personal fulfillment.

People-pleasing is often mistaken for kindness. But true kindness doesn't require self-erasure. People-pleasing is the tendency to shape-shift, to anticipate others' needs, agree when we disagree, and stay quiet to avoid conflict. It's not generosity; it's protection. A survival strategy we often learn in childhood or through trauma.

We become so attuned to how others feel that we lose track of how *we* feel. We avoid difficult conversations, delay our own dreams, and absorb responsibility that doesn't belong to us.

People-pleasing is especially common among women who are socialized to believe that harmony is more important than honesty. That saying "yes" is safer than saying "no." That being liked is more important than being respected.

But saying "yes" all the time disconnects us from our truth. It breeds resentment, exhaustion, and disconnection from our needs. Reclaiming your voice means allowing people to be disappointed. It means trusting that your worth doesn't depend on your ability to keep everyone happy.

When we stop performing politeness and start honoring our boundaries, we create room for real connection built on honesty, not appeasement.

Over-Functioning: When Doing Too Much Becomes an Identity

Over-functioning is a form of control dressed as competence. When we are over-functioning, we are the ones who always "have it handled," anticipate needs before they're spoken, and fix, manage, and smooth everything over. But beneath that constant doing is often a belief that your value comes from being needed or being busy.

Women are frequently praised for over-functioning, but without acknowledgment of the cost. We're told we're dependable, selfless, strong. But no one asks what it costs us to carry so much. And no one questions why the burden always seems to land on our shoulders.

Over-functioning is often rooted in fear. We fear that if we stop, everything will fall apart, if we ask for help, we'll look weak, and if we don't *over*achieve, we'll lose our place.

But doing more doesn't mean you *are* more. In fact, over-functioning can keep us from intimacy, from rest, from clarity. It keeps us reactive instead of intentional. Exhausted instead of empowered.

Over-functioning, taking on more, doing more, fixing everything, is often praised in women. Especially if you are the oldest daughter in a family. But it's also a sign of a deeper belief: that our worth is tied to our output. We are taught that we will never be loved or feel secure just by being ourselves—we must prove we're indispensable. Over-functioning, like perfectionism and people-pleasing, also sets us up for things like chronic fatigue and depression. We feel as though we have to be the strong one who can, and always will, carry all the weight. We start to feel as though there is no one we can count on. If we let our guard down or show vulnerability, the whole system will fall apart. It's a very lonely place to be.

Reclaiming your voice means learning to pause. To delegate. To let go. To know that your presence is powerful even when you're not performing. That being still is not being lazy, it's being wise.

Unlearning these patterns doesn't mean becoming careless, selfish, or mean. It means understanding that our value is not conditional. That rest is not laziness. That our purpose is not to carry everything, but to live fully.

Collective Healing and Breaking the Pattern

These patterns—perfectionism, people-pleasing, and over-functioning—are rarely personal quirks. They are inherited responses to cultural expectations, family dynamics, and social conditioning. They're what many of us witnessed in our mothers, grandmothers, teachers, and role models. We saw women praised for self-sacrifice and punished for self-expression. We saw love earned through performance and safety maintained by silence.

But something is shifting. More and more women are choosing to disrupt these cycles. We are raising daughters who are encouraged to be bold rather than compliant. We are raising sons to understand that emotional labor is not gendered. And we are healing ourselves not just for our own freedom, but for the generations coming after us.

It's in naming these patterns that we loosen their grip. It's in sharing our stories that we realize we're not alone. And it's in building new models of leadership, love, and success, that we re-define what it means to live unmuted.

Healing is not just personal, it's political. Every time a woman rests without guilt, says no without apology, or names her needs without shame, she challenges a system that told her she had to earn her worth. This is how change begins. Not with permission, but with one unmuted voice at a time.

Letting Go of Roles That Don't Fit

What happens when the roles we were given don't reflect who we are? When we recognize that expectations of "mother," "part-ner," "leader," "daughter," "good girl" may be cages, not callings?

Letting go of roles doesn't mean walking away from responsi-bility. It means walking toward authenticity. It means asking, "Is this still true for me?" and having the courage to adjust.

Michelle Obama has spoken openly about the tension between societal expectations and her personal aspirations. Before becom-ing First Lady, she was a Harvard-educated attorney and hospital executive, yet once in the White House, she was often reduced to the role of "wife" or "mom-in-chief." While she embraced motherhood and family with pride, she also resisted the notion that these roles defined her entirely. In her memoir *Becoming*, she reflects on how difficult it was to reconcile her ambitions with the narrow lanes available to women in the public eye. Rather than shrink herself to fit a predefined mold, she expanded her role as first lady by using her platform to champion education, health, and leadership for girls and women globally. Her story reminds us that letting go of roles doesn't necessarily mean walking away. It can be about reshaping roles into something that reflects who we really are.

Letting go also means grieving. Sometimes we hold on not be-cause something fits, but because it's familiar. Releasing it may feel like a loss but on the other side is expansion. That's not to say that getting to expansion is easy. It's a journey that we undertake knowingly and by keeping our eyes wide open to the process.

Redefining Ambition, Beauty, and Success

For too long, ambition was coded masculine. For women, to be driven was to be cold. To want more was to be too much. But ambition, when it's aligned with values, is sacred. I think it helps to move us closer to purpose.

Hyacinth Tucker, a Maryland-based Army veteran, started washing laundry as a small side job during a financially difficult time in 2022. After earning $20 helping a friend, she realized the potential in the $16 billion U.S. laundry industry and launched her own business, the Laundry Basket. Despite initial financial challenges, Tucker expanded aggressively, gaining clients across the D.C. and northern Virginia region. Her company now processes up to 7,000 pounds of laundry monthly and partners with local charities.

Rahama Wright turned her compassion into commerce. As a Peace Corps volunteer in Mali, she watched women labor invisibly over shea butter—an ingredient beloved abroad yet undervalued at home. Shea Yeleen allowed her to reframe beauty as social justice. By creating women-led cooperatives across Ghana, Burkina Faso, and Mali, Wright transformed shea butter into both balm and livelihood. Her products became a conduit for women's independence, their stories carried across borders with every natural balm and soap. In a world that often limits beauty to surface value, she showed that true beauty begins with empowerment, intention, and the rewriting of economic narratives.

Redefining beauty means seeing power in presence, not polish. It means making space for aging, scars, softness, style. It means refusing to treat our bodies as projects.

Success, too, must be reclaimed. Not as a title or a number, but as alignment. As peace. As the ability to live your truth without apology.

How We Talk to Girls

The work of redefining ambition, beauty, and success doesn't begin in adulthood. It begins in childhood, in how we speak to the next generation. Too often, girls are told they will be great mothers, but not great leaders. They're praised for being pretty, not for being smart. They're told they're "not good at math," or "more emotional" than boys, planting seeds of doubt that grow into self-limiting beliefs instead of the very real skill of being able to handle emotions in a healthy way. We also do a disservice to boys. While they have emotions just like us, they are less likely to develop the skills to handle strong emotions like anger which turns into rage and leads to men committing the vast majority of violent crimes.

We teach girls to seek approval, not agency. To be pleasant, not powerful. And even when we encourage their dreams, we sometimes frame ambition as a burden rather than a birthright. For example: we expect boys to succeed. It's their birthright. We say, "He's going to be a doctor." While we say to girls, "You can be a doctor if you work hard."

This kind of messaging creates an invisible ceiling long before girls enter the workforce. It teaches them that success is not a given, it's conditional. Their worth and chances of success are rooted in how they're seen, not who they are. Redefining power means changing these narratives. It means telling girls that their minds matter as much as their manners. That they can be beautiful and brilliant. They can be ambitious and lead with both heart and strength—which are complementary, not contradictory, qualities. It means modeling confidence, curiosity, and courage in our own lives, so they grow up knowing they never have to choose between being accepted and being themselves.

When We Dismiss Girls' Voices

It starts small. A girl speaks up at the dinner table and is talked over. She shares an idea in class and it's attributed to someone else. She raises a concern and is told she's being too sensitive.

From a young age, many girls are taught that their input is secondary if not completely unimportant. That their observations are less valid, their feelings less trustworthy, their voices less valuable. This dismissal isn't always malicious. Often, it's unconscious, a result of generations of conditioning about whose voices matter most.

But the impact is real. Each interruption, each eyeroll, each instance of being ignored sends the same message: Your voice is inconvenient. Your perspective is expendable.

And so many girls, over time, stop raising their hands. Stop asking questions. Stop offering insight. Not because they have nothing to say but because they've learned it won't be heard.

Undoing this pattern means paying attention. It means listening when girls speak. Asking their opinions. Taking their ideas seriously. It means treating their voices as sources of wisdom, not disruptions.

Because when a girl knows her voice is heard, she learns that her voice has power. And from that power, she begins to lead.

How We Talk to Boys

Just as girls are handed a script of softness and silence, boys are often handed one of toughness and domination. From an early age, boys are told not to cry, not to "act like a girl," to be strong, stoic, and assertive. When a boy teases a girl, pulls her hair, or shows aggression, adults often excuse it with, "It just means he likes you." This is another way of proactively silencing girls and women. If they speak up about bullying or abuse, they learn early on that excuses will be made for the bullies and abusers.

What message does that send? That power looks like control. That affection is expressed through dominance. That girls should accept discomfort as a sign of desirability. And that boys don't need to be held accountable because "boys will be boys."

This language does harm on all sides. It teaches boys that their feelings make them weak and less than. That connection must come at someone else's expense. It tells them that girls should silently tolerate harm in the name of love, or to ensure their own safety.

Rewriting the rules means offering boys new scripts. Encouraging empathy. Rewarding emotional expression. Teaching them that true strength lies in accountability, not aggression. That real power supports and uplifts. It doesn't suppress or diminish. And that girls' ambitions, voices and contributions don't need to be sacrificed to theirs.

Because if we want to raise girls who use their voices, we must also raise boys who respect them. We must raise boys and teach men to listen to girls and women. Not placate but actually listen. If we want to create a culture where power is shared and not hoarded, we must start by changing the words we use and the values we pass on to all our children.

The Words We Use, the Phrases We Repeat

Language is never neutral. It reflects and reinforces the culture we live in and in that culture, the way we talk about girls, women, and harm done to them often centers comfort over clarity, the passive over the active, and silence over accountability.

We tell little girls they're *"too bossy"* instead of *"natural leaders,"* the words used for boys. We describe a confident woman as *"intimidating"* or *"cold,"* while her male counterpart is *"commanding"* or *"strong."* In classrooms and boardrooms, girls are *"talkative"* or *"chatty,"* while boys are *"expressive"* or *"insightful."* Even praise is often coated in limitation: she's "pretty and smart," "a great multitasker," "nurturing" compliments that imply caretaking, compatibility, and not too much ambition.

We also see this distortion in how we describe harm. Consider how we talk about domestic violence. In the media, we hear that *"she was found dead"* rather than *"he killed her." "She was in an abu-*

sive relationship" instead of *"her partner was abusive."* These phrases remove the actor from the action and therefore avoid naming men as perpetrators. They distance the reader from the reality and they subtly shift focus to the victim's experience instead of the perpetrator's behavior. This linguistic framing protects the aggressor, blurs accountability, and perpetuates the myth that violence is private, isolated, or mutual.

In legal terminology, the problem compounds. Terms like *"domestic disturbance"* or *"family dispute"* often replace what is, in fact, *physical assault.* Protective orders may be referred to as *"no-contact orders,"* which softens their urgent and necessary purpose. When abuse survivors are cross-examined in court, they are often asked about how they *"provoked"* the violence or why they stayed, rarely about the pattern of coercion or fear they endured. This legal language coded, impersonal, and at times accusatory can retraumatize victims and obscure the truth in favor of procedural neutrality.

To unlearn these patterns, we must start by naming them. We must replace euphemism with honesty. Replace passivity with action. Say *"He abused her,"* not *"She was abused."* Say *"She was murdered by her husband,"* not *"She died in a domestic incident."* Say *"She left because she feared for her life,"* not *"She broke up with him over a fight."*

And we must model this clarity in every setting: at home, in schools, in workplaces, and on the air. It's about how mothers *and* fathers speak to both boys and girls. When we speak differently, we teach differently. We raise children who learn that respect is not gendered. We create media that informs without distorting. We shape laws that center truth over tradition.

Because words matter. They shape how we interpret the world, how we assign blame or compassion, and how we either uphold or dismantle systems of power. If we want to redefine power, we must also redefine how we speak about it.

Language shapes perception. It reveals what we believe, what we prioritize, and who holds power. Too often, the words we use to describe girls, women, and acts of harm reflect deeply embedded biases that uphold silence and shield accountability.

Story

I was the little girl who wrote. I was composing stories and poems before I could write them down myself. My mother would jot them down for me. As soon as I could hold a pencil, I wrote them down for myself and did not stop. At least, not for a long time. The one constant in my life was my writing. Anyone who knew me knew that.

Fast forward. I'm married with a couple little kids and my old friend Mimi visits us in our home in New York's Hudson Valley. As we stroll through the back yard, she asks what I'm writing. Last I saw her, I was still at Columbia University getting my MFA in fiction, working on a collection of stories. "Well," I said, "I'm not really writing these days. I'm busy with my teaching and the kids. Dan is the writer in the family." He was working on a novel. The expression on Mimi's face stopped me in my tracks. She turned to face me and peered into my face, confused. "You're not writing?"

I had voluntarily muted myself right around when I married my now-ex-husband. He was a writer too, and a shattering incident in Grand Central Station became the pivot point. I could have ended the relationship, postponed the wedding until we tried couples therapy, or move forward as if nothing had happened. Can you guess which I chose?

It was that day when I met his train that it hit me—he would not be okay if I had success as a writer before he did. Or, perhaps, at all. When I told him I'd just had a story accepted by a literary journal—before he had one accepted—his reaction was not one of joy for me. There were no hugs, no congratulations. It's true that his rageful tantrum in the middle of 42nd St. was not directed at me, per se, but at "life" and the "unfairness of things." It's true that he "never asked me to stop writing." But the choice was clear. Peace and moving ahead with the imminent wedding

(4 months away) or cataclysmic upheaval. I guess my brain just made the choice for me, protecting me as best it knew how.

I spent 25 years muted, rationalizing my decision not to write in countless ways. Demanding work schedule, the kids, taking care of countless things that left me exhausted by 10 p.m. Of course, he managed to write every day. Had I understood then that the only reason he could do that was because I was taking care of the other stuff that made his life run smoothly, I might have woken up sooner.

I have gone through many stages of grief and regret about those lost 25 years. I understand that I was gaslit by the patriarchy into thinking my silence was not just okay, but appropriate. But I'm good now. And writing.

Within 24 hours of telling my husband I was leaving our marriage, I had written an entire short story. It poured out of me like water through a culvert after a weeklong rain.

Chapter 6:

Collective Voice, Collective Power

"The connections between and among women are the most feared, the most problematic, and the most potentially transforming force on the planet"
— Adrienne Rich

There is a revolution happening and it's powered by women who are no longer waiting for permission to lead, speak, or rise. In homes, in workplaces, and on global stages, women are challenging the narrative that we must go it alone. We are rewriting the story that leadership is a solo act and power is a scarce resource. Instead, we are proving that when women rise together, we rise stronger.

How Women Rise Together

We've long been fed the idea that there's only room for one woman at the top, that power is a pie with only so many slices. But the truth is, power multiplies when it's shared. The success of one woman doesn't diminish another's; it expands what's possible for all of us.

Women have always found ways to rise, even when systems tried to hold us down. But the most powerful moments of change have never happened in isolation. They happen when women rise *together*. From grassroots activism to intergenerational mentorship, from shared caregiving to global feminist movements, we have seen what's possible when individual voices unite into a collective roar.

Rising together means creating spaces where women are seen, heard, and supported, not judged or ranked. In these spaces, women celebrate one another's stories and success rather than competing for a narrow version of power that was never designed with us in mind. It's understanding that our freedom is tied to each other's, and that collective liberation starts with solidarity.

But rising together doesn't mean we always agree—or need to. True solidarity allows space for complexity and difference. It invites dialogue, not conformity. And it thrives on trust, not perfection.

Collective power isn't a slogan. It's a strategy. It's what happens when we refuse to compete for one seat allotted for us at the table—and instead build longer tables. When we share resources, amplify each other's voices, and celebrate wins that aren't our own. It's mentorship. It's advocacy. It's sisterhood in action.

When women rise together, we normalize ambition. We normalize boundary-setting. We normalize emotional honesty and bold ideas. By not standing alone, we make it harder for systems to dismiss us.

For too long, women were told to compete with men and with each other. To view each other as threats instead of allies. This scarcity mindset was no accident. It was a function of systems that benefited from our division.

Many of us were taught to believe there's room for only one woman at the table or in the spotlight. This manufactured scarcity trains us to compare, compete, and even withhold support. The result? We disconnect from each other and also from ourselves. But competition is an intentional distraction, especially among women who have long been underrepresented in decision-making spaces.

Collaboration is our natural strength. It's how women have always survived and thrived, through community care, shared wisdom, and relational intelligence. When we collaborate, we model a different kind of power. One that is sustainable, creative, and expansive.

When we choose collaboration, we're not avoiding excellence or ambition. We're redefining what winning looks like. It means believing that our successes are interconnected, that lifting others is not a detour from our path, but the very thing that clears the way.

Collaboration reclaims our power. It says: I don't need to win alone. We can rise *together*. Collaboration looks like shared credit, mutual mentorship, resource-sharing, and building systems that benefit *everyone*, not just the most visible. I'm not advocating that we erase individual voices—quite the opposite. Each unique voice is a significant and valuable voice. But let's not forget the strength we create when we work, share, talk, and create together.

Whether in boardrooms or legislatures, classrooms or book clubs, kitchens or communities, collaboration invites us to move differently. It teaches us to ask: How can I support you? How can we win together? How can we create something bigger than any of us could alone?

Collaboration is not a luxury; it's a leadership strategy. It's not weakness, it's wisdom.

Solidarity Across Difference

It's one thing to unite with women who look like us, live like us, or think like us. But true collective power asks more. It asks us to reach across lines of race, class, sexuality, ability, age, religion, and geography and choose expansive, inclusive solidarity. It asks us to listen, learn, and sometimes unlearn. It asks us to center the voices of those historically pushed to the margins. It means acknowledging privilege where it exists and redistributing access, credit, and opportunity.

Solidarity across differences acknowledges that not all women experience womanhood in the same way. A white woman's experience in the workplace is not the same as the experience of a Black or Indigenous woman. A cisgender woman's story will differ from that of a trans woman. Real power comes from making space for those stories not just in theory, but in action. There is room for us all.

Intersectionality, a term coined by legal scholar Kimberlé Crenshaw, reminds us that systems of oppression overlap. Gender doesn't exist in a vacuum. When we ignore these intersections, we fail to build inclusive power. But when we honor them, we build something much stronger: a movement grounded in justice and led by diverse voices.

Solidarity isn't always comfortable. It asks us to stay in the room when the conversation gets hard. It asks us to believe women of color. To center marginalized voices. To unlearn patterns of saviorism or silence. True solidarity is not performative, it's practiced.

Collective power that doesn't include all women isn't collective at all. Our liberation is bound together. And so is our responsibility.

Systemic change doesn't happen just because we raise awareness. It happens when we leverage our collective voice to demand new systems, new policies, and new norms. It asks us to move from insight to action.

For systemic change to happen, we must look beyond individual empowerment and address the cultural and institutional structures that keep power unequal. This includes everything from pay equity to representation, parental leave to healthcare, education to safety.

And this includes gender-based violence.

Collective Power Against Gender-Based Violence

Gender-based violence is one of the most pervasive and least addressed manifestations of power imbalance in our world. It includes physical, sexual, emotional, and economic abuse, and it thrives in silence, shame, and systems that fail to protect.

This isn't just a personal issue, it's a public crisis. From domestic violence to workplace harassment, from femicide to digital abuse, women face threats that are routinely minimized or dismissed. And those at the intersections, Black women, Indigenous women, trans women, disabled women, face even greater vulnerability.

The scope is staggering:

- Nearly 1 in 3 women globally (30%) experience physical and/or sexual violence perpetrated by men. This number is likely much higher as women often do not report. Violence goes underreported not because women are unwilling to seek justice, but because the personal cost of speaking out often feels greater than the potential benefit. Fear, stigma, systemic failures, and cultural silencing combine to keep women muted. The responsibility lies with the perpetrators and with the structures that protect them, not with the women who survive.

- Over 370 million girls and women, 1 in 8 globally, have been raped or sexually assaulted before turning 18.

- An average of 140 women and girls are killed daily by a partner or family member worldwide, totaling over 51,000 deaths annually.

- In the U.S., 1 in 4 women has experienced intimate partner violence. Native American women are more than twice as likely to experience violence. And femicide is the leading cause of death for pregnant and postpartum women.

When women speak up about abuse and are not believed, when survivors are retraumatized by the very systems meant to support them, when the burden of proof outweighs the benefit of protection, that is not justice. That is the cost of silence codified into culture.

Collective voice means believing survivors. It means advocating for stronger laws, trauma-informed responses, and prevention rooted in education, not fear. It means calling out the media when it sensationalizes harm but silences healing. It means refusing to normalize violence in any form from the jokes we tolerate to the institutions we fund and using collective action and our votes to reform the justice system so that more men are held accountable.

We are not powerless. When we speak together, move together, and demand better together, we become the system. And we begin to change it. I firmly believe this and at the same time feel powerless myself. I feel overwhelmed and hopeless at times. When I read the statistics, see the news stories and listen to women I know who have experienced, first the abuse and then the lack of support and re-traumatization of the system, I feel anger and rage. It can be paralyzing. Part of why I wanted to write this book stems from that feeling of helplessness. What can I do? I'm just one person.

Systemic change requires systemic courage. And that means using our collective power not just to raise awareness, but to demand accountability. It means standing beside those whose voices have been silenced and amplifying them until the system is forced to listen.

In 2015, Chanel Miller was sexually assaulted by Brock Turner, a Stanford University student. For months, she was known only as "Emily Doe" in court documents and media reports. The justice system, the university, and the public conversation focused more on the future of the perpetrator than on the harm done to her. The judge handed down a sentence of only six months, citing concern for Turner's potential.

Chanel's voice was almost erased. Yet she reclaimed it. In a powerful victim impact statement read in court, she spoke not just for herself but for countless others whose stories were minimized. That statement went viral, read by millions, and became a rallying cry against the silencing of survivors. Later, she revealed her name publicly in her memoir, *Know My Name*. By doing so, she shifted the narrative from anonymity and shame to strength and agency.

Intergenerational Collaboration

One of the most powerful and often overlooked forms of collective strength comes through intergenerational collaboration. When younger and older women come together, each with their distinct wisdom and perspectives, we create a multigenerational ecosystem of resilience and knowledge. I am inspired and encouraged by the younger generations.

Younger generations bring innovation, digital fluency, and a deep desire to disrupt outdated systems. Older generations offer lived experience, institutional memory, and the long view of change. When we listen to one another, when we create space to both teach and learn, we build bridges, not silos.

Mentorship doesn't have to be top-down. In today's world, reverse mentorship and mutual learning can transform how we lead, organize, and build community. Intergenerational collaboration models a future that isn't divided by age but connected by purpose.

Allyship Across Genders

While *Unmuted* centers women's experiences, collective power requires that we also invite men into the conversation *not* to center them, but to include them as partners in dismantling patriarchal systems that harm everyone.

Allyship across genders means men doing the work to unlearn toxic masculinity, to listen without defensiveness, and to take responsibility without needing applause. It's men choosing to yield power, amplify women's voices, and show up in solidarity especially when it's uncomfortable.

Allyship isn't about speaking for women. It's about making space, taking accountability, and committing to equity, not to give lip service to it as a buzzword but to live it as a daily practice. In organizations, this looks like transparent promotion policies, equitable parental leave, and a willingness to hear and act on feedback about culture. In families, it looks like sharing emotional and physical labor. In relationships, it looks like respect, curiosity, and co-creation.

When men support women's voices, not out of charity but out of shared humanity, the paradigm begins to shift away from dominance and toward dignity.

Collective Wins

Collective power isn't just a concept. It's a proven force. Across history and geography, women's movements have created seismic change by organizing together.

- The women-led movement for reproductive rights in Argentina culminated in the legalization of abortion after decades of resistance and protest. Their green bandanas became a global symbol of feminist resistance.

- In Liberia, women organized a nonviolent protest movement, led by Leymah Gbowee, that helped end a brutal civil war. Dressed in white, they prayed and protested until peace negotiations were held. Their story is a testament to what happens when women refuse to be silent.

- Black Lives Matter, co-founded by women including Patrisse Cullors and Alicia Garza, shows the intersectional power of Black women's leadership and the global reach of grassroots organizing.

- Mutual aid networks that emerged during the COVID-19 pandemic were often led by women, especially women of color, who stepped in to fill gaps left by failing systems, offering food, medical access, and support when institutions fell short.

These are not isolated wins. They are proof that when women come together, not in competition, but in collective clarity, we change lives, laws, and legacies.

A Reflection on Burnout in Activism

The fight for justice is relentless and so are the demands on those who lead it. Burnout in activist spaces is real, especially for women who are expected to be endlessly available, emotionally resilient, and always "on."

Activist burnout doesn't just come from the work itself. It comes from navigating systems that resist change, from facing backlash or erasure, from carrying the emotional weight of entire communities, and from making personal sacrifices to stay in the fight. A fight that overwhelmingly benefits men.

Acknowledging burnout isn't a weakness. Rest is resistance. Boundaries are strategy. Replenishment is necessary for sustainability. Collective care must be part of collective power.

We need systems that nourish us while we build systems that liberate us. And we must remember: it's not just okay to step back, it's essential. The work will continue because we are not doing it alone.

Though it no longer exists, Megan Park started Putting Women in Their Place (PWITP) in 2017 out of a desire to help women. She was responding directly to the 2016 election and the defeat of a highly credible, experienced, and educated woman candidate by a white man with none of those qualities. Park wanted to support women to enter political races they have traditionally been kept out of due to the patriarchal tradition of "it's always been this way." When Hilary Clinton ran for president, very few women were running for political office of any kind, and this was the first time a woman won the presidential nomination of a major party. Putting Women in Their Place meant putting women where they belong—in positions of leadership, in the halls of power.

Using her background and experience in independent film, Park committed to creating affordable campaign videos for women running for office, specifically elected positions at the beginning of the pipeline. Her "Trickle Up Theory" is that by filling school boards and town halls, by supporting women running for clerk of courts, town supervisor, and sheriff, the numbers game that is politics would shift. Park's company motto was "From the Courthouse to the Statehouse to the White House."

She networked nationwide to enlist videographers and directors to create campaign videos, giving women a platform—unmuting them so people could hear what they stood for.

Before 2017, it was very difficult for women candidates to raise money because it was so rare for women to run. Donors hesitated to invest in someone they did not think would win. This belief was due to the fact that they hadn't seen women winning. They didn't see women winning because they didn't run. In many cases, they did not run because they couldn't raise funds. A vicious, self-perpetuating cycle that kept potential women candidates muted.

Men look around the halls of power and say, "I belong here." Women have to work much   harder to get through the door. When they do, they have experiences so miserable, many give up and never run for higher office.

When there was no childcare for key town board meetings held in the evenings, the narrative became "She missed a meeting," not "How do we accommodate women board members with childcare or by scheduling meetings during the school day?"

It was not lost on Park that men do not require these accommodations. If they have children, they likely also have a wife who manages "all of that." The more women are in the political pipeline, the more they can support each other to stay the course and move on to higher offices.

Putting Women in Their Place aimed to help women leap over hurdles by giving them a voice, so that people could hear what they stood for. Social media was the perfect free platform for sharing their political objectives.

The Cost of Isolation vs. the Power of Belonging

Isolation is a strategy of suppression. We are seeing this at home here in the United States, isolating us from the rest of the world and from each other. When women are siloed, by fear, by shame, by stigma, we are easier to control and less likely to challenge the systems that hold us back. Isolation keeps us second-guessing ourselves, believing we are alone in our struggles, and disconnected from the collective strength we hold.

Belonging, on the other hand, tells us that we do not have to go it alone. That our stories are not anomalies. That our pain is shared and so is our power. When we find spaces of true belonging, we are not just affirmed, we are activated. We are reminded that our voice matters, our truth is valid, and our presence is necessary.

The cost of isolation is self-doubt, burnout, and the slow erosion of our voice. The power of belonging is courage, connection, and the collective momentum to change the world. In community, we remember that being unmuted is not just about speaking, it's about being heard, held, and joined by others who believe in a freer future for all of us.

Story

I've had a loud voice for as long as I can remember. Many Brooklyn girls are born with one. It's part of the survival kit. But being loud doesn't always mean you're heard.

I didn't shrink. I adapted. I tried to package myself in a way I thought would be more acceptable. Maybe if I wore the "smart" glasses, pulled my hair back, dressed like someone who belonged at the boardroom table, I'd be taken seriously. I wasn't pretending, but I was editing. Editing to fit into rooms that weren't built for women like me, especially the bold, intuitive, truth-telling kind.

But loss has a way of stripping away everything that doesn't matter. When I lost my infant son, Shane, I stopped waiting for someone else's approval. My voice didn't just grow louder, it grew clearer. I had something to say, and the world wasn't going to hand me a mic. I had to build my own stage and then invite every woman I knew to stand on it with me.

I used that voice to build inclusive playgrounds, to launch She Angels Foundation, and to fund and amplify the voices of other women who've been underestimated or unheard.

Today, being unmuted means honoring that little girl in Brooklyn who always knew she had something to offer and never letting her be dismissed again. My voice isn't just mine anymore. It belongs to the movement I'm building, to the women I fund, and to the world we're rewriting together.

Chapter 7:

Raising Strong Unmuted Voices – Empowering the Next Generation

"We badly need to raise our boys more like our girls."
– Gloria Steinem

Though it may take some of us until adulthood to own our voices, voice doesn't begin in adulthood. It begins at birth. We learn to apply the rules at the kitchen table, on the playground, in the classroom, and in the quiet moments when children are told explicitly or implicitly what's acceptable to feel, say, and believe. If we want to create a world where women speak freely and lead powerfully, we must start by raising children who know their voices matter.

Let's look at how we model, teach, and reinforce voice from an early age. How we speak to our children and how we listen shapes their internal sense of worth, confidence, and power.

Modeling Self-Expression at Home

Children don't just learn from what we say. They learn from what we do. When we, as adults, share our thoughts openly, set clear boundaries, and speak with compassion and conviction, we show children that using our voices authentically is not only allowed, it's essential.

Raising girls to know their voice starts with what they see and hear modeled. Modeling voice at home means saying what you need, naming your emotions, and acknowledging when you've made a mistake. It means creating space for disagreement and letting children express themselves without fear of punishment or shame. It begins when we, as adults, use our own voices clearly and unapologetically. When we demonstrate healthy boundaries, speak our truth even when it's uncomfortable, and show children that our worth isn't measured by how much we please others.

Even the specific words we use carry weight, both negative and positive.

It happens in the small, everyday moments:

- Encouraging them to share their opinions at the dinner table, even if we disagree
- Asking what *they* want rather than making decisions for them
- Affirming their anger, joy, confusion, and curiosity as valid, rather than labeling them as dramatic, emotional, or needy

A household where voice is respected becomes a training ground for future self-advocates. It teaches children that their inner world matters and that they have the right to be heard.

Raising Girls to Know and Trust Their Voices

From a young age, girls are socialized to be agreeable, accommodating, and deferential. This conditioning doesn't just silence girls, it trains them to question their instincts and doubt their worth.

We change this by encouraging girls to speak their minds, ask questions, and disagree respectfully.

We can't forget to talk to girls about ambition, success, and identity. When we tell girls they'll "make great mothers" or praise them for being pretty before we tell them they're smart, strategic, or creative, we send subtle messages about where their value lies. I am not advocating that we demonize motherhood. My point here is to be aware of taking away their choices with the language we use. When we downplay their achievements to keep them humble or tell them to smile to be likable, we reinforce that being pleasing is more important than being powerful.

Many women carry the long shadow of these early messages, struggling to claim their accomplishments without apology. They fear being seen as arrogant or ungrateful, even when they've worked hard for every success. To raise unmuted girls, we must actively counter this narrative. We must celebrate their wins, encourage them to name their strengths, and model what it looks like to own our achievements without shrinking, apologizing, or demurring.

We can help them practice self-recognition by asking, "What are you proud of today?" or saying, "You worked really hard on that, I hope you feel proud of yourself." These small shifts plant the seeds for a strong, resilient voice and an individual who has choices in life.

We must counterbalance, on a daily basis, the constant barrage of objectification of girls and women in the media, movies, television, advertising, and social media. Don't get me started on the Disney princess role model that my daughter grew up with. It was impossible to get away from it. I struggled with letting her express herself through the princess lens (which she loved) and showing her different role models.

If we want the next generation of women to lead with confidence and authenticity, we need to be cognizant of the messages, both subtle and overt, they receive about when and how it's acceptable to speak up.

But what if we flipped the script entirely? What if we taught our daughters that their thoughts, boundaries, and emotions aren't just valid, they're essential? That speaking clearly and confidently is a strength, not a flaw? And that being called "bossy" isn't something to shrink away from, but often a sign that they are stepping into their own power?

I remember this so clearly from my own childhood. I was about eight or nine years old when I found out that Diana Rigg was leaving *The Avengers*, a show I adored and looked forward to every week. I cried so hard I couldn't be consoled. I loved everything she stood for. Her character embodied everything I longed to see in myself, physicality, boldness, fearlessness. I exhibited none of those things, of course. She took up space and made no apologies for it. When my mother saw me crying, she couldn't understand. She told me how ridiculous I was being, that I was silly and too sensitive. But what I know now is that I was mourning the loss of a powerful role model before I even had the words to explain why she mattered to me.

How a father treats a mother or any partner in the home is one of the earliest and most powerful lessons about respect that a child will witness. When boys see their fathers listening to, valuing, and honoring the voices of the women in their lives, it shapes their understanding of what healthy, respectful relationships look like. And when girls witness their mothers being treated as equals, heard, supported, and respected, they learn that their own voices deserve that same respect, both now and in the future. In this way, home becomes the first stage where the value of women's voices is either affirmed or quietly diminished.

We don't empower girls by telling them to be confident, we empower them by *listening* when they already are. By honoring their leadership, even when it's messy. And by making sure their voices are heard in the moments when it matters most.

Raising Boys to Honor and Support Girls' Voices

Unmuting the next generation isn't just about teaching girls to speak, it's about teaching boys to listen, respect, and make space.

Boys are often raised with narrow definitions of strength, stoicism, dominance, control. Emotional expression is discouraged, while entitlement is sometimes rewarded. And while girls are told to be accommodating, boys are given permission to interrupt, dominate, and dismiss.

We shift this by teaching boys that leadership includes listening. That respect means valuing perspectives different from their own. That power is not taken, it's shared.

We tell girls, *"Don't make a scene," "Be nice," "Smile,"* and *"Let him go first."* We reward politeness over self-expression.

These phrases normalize harm and teach girls that being hurt or disrespected is a sign of affection and that they should endure discomfort to be desired. It also teaches boys that acting out is acceptable if it comes from a place of "liking." The impact? Girls internalize silence. Boys internalize entitlement.

This also teaches boys that care is expressed through control. Instead, we must teach that kindness and strength are not opposites. That real connection is built on consent, mutuality, and care.

We must show boys that vulnerability is not weakness and that supporting others doesn't diminish their worth, it deepens it. When boys learn to honor the voices of girls, we build a future where collaboration, not dominance, is the standard.

Raising boys to support girls' voices isn't only about teaching them to be polite or to step aside in conversations. It's about instilling in them a deep respect for women's experiences and a willingness to believe those experiences, especially when they reveal hard, uncomfortable truths.

For generations, when women have spoken up about being harassed, stalked, or abused, their voices have been met with suspicion, dismissal, accusation, or outright disbelief. "Are you sure that's what happened?" "Maybe you're overreacting." "What did you do to make him mad?" "He's such a nice guy; he wouldn't do that." These aren't just harmless doubts. This pattern of disbelief has silenced women in courtrooms, police stations, workplaces, and even within their own families. And it allows harm to continue unchecked. Whether you agree with releasing the Epstein files (big news as I write this), or not, if we believed the women who have already come forward and testified, we wouldn't need the files!

When we raise boys to listen deeply and believe women when they share their lived experiences, we begin to dismantle the cultural narratives that protect abusers and discredit survivors. We teach boys that their role isn't to question or defend harmful behavior, it's to stand beside women, to advocate for them, and to help create spaces where their voices are heard and trusted.

Because when a woman says, "I feel unsafe," she shouldn't have to prove it. And when she speaks her truth, she should never have to shout just to be believed.

While teaching girls to use their voices, it's also important to raise boys who respect, support, and make space for those voices. Boys, too, are socialized into a narrow understanding of power. If we want to build a more equitable future, we must raise boys who see collaboration, emotional intelligence, and humility as leadership qualities, not weaknesses.

We can start by helping boys understand that leadership isn't about being the loudest voice in the room but about listening deeply and honoring the voices around them. It's teaching them to recognize when they're taking up space and how to step back so others can shine. It's showing them that strength includes empathy, and that supporting others doesn't diminish their own power—it strengthens it.

When boys grow up understanding that the success of girls and women doesn't threaten their own, we begin to break the cycles that have kept true equality out of reach. And in doing so, we raise a generation of men who lead not by silencing others, but by lifting them up.

As parents, mentors, and role models, it's not enough to tell boys to "be respectful." We must actively show them what it looks like to believe and respect women, to advocate for them when their voices are dismissed, and to stand up against the systems that silence them.

The conversations we have at home are a strong beginning. The male role models they see on a regular basis are hugely important, as are the moments when we teach our sons that empathy is strength, that consent is non-negotiable, and that true leadership means creating space for others to rise.

If we're serious about raising boys to support and respect the voices of girls and women, we also have to confront the cultural narratives they're exposed to every day. From advertising to movies, music, and even casual conversations, we live in a society that relentlessly objectifies women and girls, reducing them to appearances, body parts, and ideals to be consumed rather than whole people to be respected. Social media multiplies these effects a thousand-fold.

This objectification isn't harmless; it shapes how boys view girls and, more dangerously, how they believe girls *should* behave. When women and girls are portrayed as prizes to be won, obstacles to be conquered, or background characters in someone else's story, it reinforces the idea that their value lies in how they look and how much they accommodate others, not in their ideas, leadership, or boundaries.

And when harm occurs, when girls are harassed, stalked, or abused, the cultural reflex is to question *her* choices: What was she wearing? Why was she there? Did she lead him on? Or the dreaded attitude that boys simply can't help themselves. What an insult to boys! The burden falls squarely on the shoulders of women and girls to protect themselves, dress appropriately, and avoid danger, while far less attention is given to teaching boys and men not to objectify, dominate, or harm in the first place.

We have to flip that narrative. We must raise boys to recognize the humanity, complexity, and sovereignty of every girl and woman they encounter. To teach them that respect isn't conditional. That a woman's body is never a commodity. And that their role is not to control or consume girls and women, but to listen, support, and stand alongside them as equals.

Because until we dismantle the objectification of women in our media, our language, and our expectations, we will continue to raise generations who believe that power looks like control and that girls must bear the weight of keeping themselves safe.

True change begins when we stop asking girls to shrink themselves and start asking boys to expand their understanding of respect, humanity, and shared power.

Because when boys learn to support, not suppress, the voices of girls and women, we don't just raise better men. We build a safer future for women.

Listening to Our Children

One of the most powerful ways to validate a child's voice is simply to listen. Not just hearing their words, but making space for their experiences, perspectives, and emotions without immediate correction, dismissal, or judgment.

When we listen deeply, we communicate: "You matter. Your voice matters." And often, in those moments of genuine listening, we uncover things that deserve our attention. A fear that's gone unnoticed. A boundary that's been crossed. A spark of creativity that needs nurturing. Listening becomes a form of protection, prevention, connection, and empowerment.

Too often, children, especially girls, are talked over, interrupted, or corrected before they can finish their thoughts. And boys are expected to shrug off their feelings or stay silent. By being present and receptive, we send a message that their thoughts are welcome, their boundaries respected, and their insights important. We can make sure they know that when they show sadness or other emotions, their feelings are valid and important.

Listening isn't passive. It's active work. It requires patience, presence, and a willingness to slow down. But when we do, we help children build the confidence to speak and the self-trust to believe that what they say matters.

Breaking Generational Cycles of Silence

Many of us grew up in households where voice was not encouraged, children were expected to be "seen and not heard," disagreement was disrespect, and speaking up led to punishment or withdrawal. That was definitely true for me growing up in the 60s and 70s. And girls were especially supposed to be seen and not heard.

These patterns don't dissolve on their own. They require conscious interruption. When we choose to parent differently—to listen more, punish less, and invite open dialogue—we begin to rewrite the narrative.

I'm not naïve enough to think we have to be perfect as parents. It's more about being aware. It's about asking ourselves: "What did I need to hear when I was young?" and then offering that to the children in our lives. Whether we are parents, caregivers, mentors, or teachers, we all have the power to disrupt silence and nurture voice.

To raise unmuted children, we must start by unmuting ourselves. We must heal the parts of us that were told to stay small, quiet, and agreeable and lead from the part that knows truth is worth speaking. Not just for our sake, but for the generations who are watching, listening, and learning from us every day.

Story

At the first financial firm I joined, I learned early on what it felt like to be excluded. I remember sitting at my cubicle as several male colleagues prepared to leave for golf with our manager. Another male peer who had not been part of the original plans, was invited on the spot. I was sitting right there, visible yet invisible excluded from formal networking that shapes careers.

Years later, when I joined a new firm. I came in with strong credentials and production numbers. But when I arrived, no one went out of their way to introduce themselves. There were no welcome lunches, no coffees, not even small gestures of inclusion. At the time, this didn't matter nor did I think I was being treated a certain way until years later, when a new male hire came onboard. He was someone with similar production to mine, but who looked the part. He had the physical presence and appearance of a stereotypical associate in the wealth management industry. 6ft+ white male in his late 50s. Within a week, I noticed that many others in the office had introduced themselves to him. People invited him to lunches, made warm introductions, and celebrated his arrival. I had done the same work, in the same role, with the same potential, but I didn't look like who they expected to succeed and they didn't want to sit at my table.

Chapter 8:

Living Unmuted

*"Every woman's success should be an inspiration to another.
We're strongest when we cheer each other on."*
– Serena Williams

Living unmuted isn't just about finding your voice, it's about using it in real life, where decisions are made, relationships are shaped, and communities are built. It's about turning self-awareness into action. Power, after all, is not an abstract ideal. It's something we practice every day in how we speak, show up, and stand for what matters.

Living in Alignment with Voice and Values

Living in alignment means that the values you hold inside are visible in choices, your boundaries, and your behaviors. It means showing up with consistency and integrity, even when it's inconvenient or unpopular. The gap between what we believe and how we behave is where much of our inner conflict lives. Closing that gap is a lifelong practice and one of the most powerful ways to reclaim agency. While I feel as though I've closed the gap significantly for me over the years, there are still times when I catch myself living in between my values and my choices.

Alignment doesn't equal perfection. It means presence. I tell many of my clients to be present not perfect. It's knowing that when you say yes, it's a true yes. That when you speak up, it's from a place of purpose, not performance. That when you make a decision, it's guided by what you stand for and not what others expect.

There have been times when I've fallen into the "do what others expect of me" category but for the most part, I do what feels right for me. Especially as I get older.

Everyday Activism and Quiet Revolutions

Not everyone is called to protest or change policy, but every woman has the power to lead a quiet revolution. Everyday activism is found in the small, consistent ways we challenge the norms that silence or shrink us and others.

Correcting someone when they mispronounce your name. Mentoring the next generation of women leaders. Making choices that reflect your worth, whether that's negotiating a raise, walking away from a toxic relationship, or simply speaking up when it would be easier to stay silent.

Every time we say, "This isn't okay" or "This matters," call out injustice, and learn the insidious signs of gaslighting and control, we chip away at a system that relies on our compliance. Every time we model healthy boundaries, advocate for inclusion, and champion women's collective power, we are part of something bigger than ourselves. And when we do it together, that quiet revolution grows louder.

Owning Our Impact in Work, Family, and Community

Too often, women are conditioned to downplay their impact, to be modest, deferential, or self-erasing. When I talk about impact, I am not talking about ego. I'm talking about responsibility. We shape the environments we inhabit, whether we realize it or not.

The question is not *if* we have influence, but *how* we choose to use it.

In the workplace, that might mean leading with empathy instead of fear. At home, it could mean raising children who know their voices matter. In community spaces, it might mean being the person who ensures everyone is heard.

We don't have to do it all. We just have to do what matters with intention. I work with my clients on intentions all the time. I'll ask them, "What was your intention when you said that?" or "When you start that conversation, what's the intention you want to lead with?" And I ask myself those same questions. I'm fallible and sometimes I lose my intention along the way, but I do believe that asking what my intention is before I take action or begin a conversation, especially a tough one, is helpful and productive. Intention matters. A voice without intention can fade into the background, but a voice rooted in clarity and purpose becomes undeniable. When we speak with intention, our words are no longer scattered—they become focused energy, carrying the power to influence hearts, shift culture, and demand justice. Voice with intention does not need to be the loudest in the room. Its strength comes from conviction, from knowing what must be said and why it matters. That kind of voice can move mountains, not through sheer volume, but through the unstoppable force of truth spoken with purpose.

Conflict and the Courage to Speak

When we reclaim our voices, we don't seek out conflict, but we don't want to avoid conflict at the cost of our integrity. We don't need to prove others wrong or always be right. We want to create clarity, connection, and accountability.

When we speak honestly, especially in tough moments, we open the door to understanding and resolution. Redefining what it means to raise our voices means seeing communication not as a weapon, but as a bridge. It's the willingness to ask hard questions, to challenge respectfully, and to stay engaged even when it's uncomfortable.

Don't get me wrong. Not everyone will welcome your voice. Some will challenge it, and others will try to silence you. That's okay. Speaking up with courage isn't the same as creating conflict, though it may result in some momentary discourse or pushbacks (you're being difficult'). In fact, it's often the first step toward defusing real conflict. Silence might feel safer in the moment, but it rarely builds trust. The long-term costs of unspoken resentment, misunderstanding, or misalignment are far greater than the cost of courage in the face of challenge.

Using your voice despite the risk of conflict doesn't mean you have to choose a side or escalate tension. What helps is to ask yourself, "What's the truth that's not being spoken here? What outcome am I hoping for? What bridge can I build?"

When we reframe speaking up as a way to find solutions, not just air frustrations, we invite transformation. We shift from confrontation to co-creation and defensiveness to dialogue. And in doing so, we redefine conflict as a space for growth, not a threat to peace. Conflict and discourse are not the same. Conflict is fueled by opposition and the desire to win; it often escalates through defensiveness, blame, and the silencing of one side by the other. Discourse, on the other hand, is fueled by curiosity and the desire to understand; it creates space for multiple perspectives, even when disagreement remains. Conflict seeks to dominate. Discourse seeks to connect. Conflict often mutes voices. Discourse invites them.

Voice becomes power when it's used not just to speak but to listen, to repair, and to lead with clarity.

I recently had a conversation with a long-time friend I felt wasn't as invested in our relationship as I was. When I brought it up, she seemed to shut down emotionally. I was hurt and saddened by her reaction, but that is the chance I took. My intention was to create a better understanding between us. I spoke my truth. She spoke hers and the friendship ended. Not where I had hoped it would go, but there were things that I felt needed to be said. I am not sorry that I said them, they were my truth. But I am sorry that she felt the need to end the friendship. Perhaps, I could have done more. I'm certainly not perfect. But it wasn't meant to be.

The Power of Listening to Others and Honoring Difference

Just as finding our voices is central to living unmuted, so is learning how to listen—really listen. Listening is not passive. It's an action that involves presence, humility, and respect. It's how we make space for others' truths without needing to rush in with our own.

In conflict, listening can be disarming. When we listen, the other person feels seen and understood, which in turn opens the door for resolution. But listening is more than a conflict-resolution tool, it's a form of solidarity.

When women listen to one another without judgment or comparison, we create space for difference. Not all of us walk the same path. We have different identities, values, perspectives, and life experiences. True solidarity is about seeing and respecting one another fully, not demanding sameness.

When men truly listen to women, it opens the door to deeper understanding and connection, laying the foundation for meaningful solidarity between genders. Listening does not mean we must agree. Validating does not mean we must be able to relate. Listening is how we say, "Your story matters. Even if it's not mine." This is empathy.

When we learn to hold space for voices different from our own, we expand our capacity for empathy and leadership. We also build a culture where unmuting doesn't mean talking over one another but rising together.

Leading, Living, and Loving Unmuted

Unmuting yourself doesn't stop once you've reclaimed your voice. It's a daily practice, a way of being. It's how you lead meetings, hold boundaries, show up in love, and walk through life. It can be laughing out loud, full-throated.

To live unmuted is to move through life with your full presence. It's to own your desires and your discomforts. To be visible not just when it's easy, but when it matters most.

It means loving with honesty, not performance. It means leading without the need for constant validation. It means showing up in your relationships, romantic, professional, or familial, with your truth intact.

Living unmuted is about choosing alignment over approval. It's about letting your values, not your fears, shape your choices. It's about making peace with being misunderstood if it means staying true to yourself.

This is how we create relationships rooted in truth, workplaces built on respect, and communities founded on equity. This is how we lead and love with intention, not obligation.

To live unmuted is to reclaim the full range of your power, not by being the loudest voice in the room, but by being the most honest one. You may still doubt yourself at times but living un-muted means refusing to stay small in the face of doubt. This is a challenge I face more often than I care to admit. Doubt and fear rear their ugly heads often when I face a new situation. For the most part, I am still able to jump in with both feet, but if I'm being honest, the doubt and fear get the best of me sometimes. However, I know I am resilient and persistent. I don't strive for perfection—that's just not in my playbook any longer. I know, at least for me, perfectionism is an exercise in futility. I is who I is!

This is what power in practice looks like. Not perfection. Not performance. But presence, persistence, and a voice that no longer waits for permission.

Helping Other Women Find Their Voices

Once we reclaim our own voices, we gain the power and the responsibility to help other women find theirs. This doesn't mean we speak for others, but we can create space where their voices are safe, welcome, and heard. I think this is why I love working with women so much. It gives me great joy and a sense of purpose when I can help another woman find, trust, and use her voice.

Women in all walks of life play a vital role in amplifying the voices of others. Teachers who encourage girls to speak their minds. Coaches who help women access clarity and confidence in pursuing their goals. Social workers and therapists who support healing from trauma. Journalists who tell women's stories. Community organizers who bring women together around shared goals. These professions and many others help women reclaim the power of their voices every day.

But you don't have to be in a helping profession to support another woman's voice. You can do it by listening without inter-rupting. By asking, "What do you think?" or "Tell me more." By recommending her for an opportunity. By standing beside her when she speaks truth to power.

When we lift up the voices of other women, we amplify our collective power. We begin to shift the culture from one of competition to one of shared strength. And that collective voice? It has the power to transform everything, from boardrooms to ballots, from policy to parenting, from silence to systemic change.

Because unmuting doesn't end with one voice. It echoes. It multiplies. It builds movements. It changes the world. I truly believe this.

There are so many stories out there, some that I have personally witnessed and others I have read about where women slowly begin sharing their challenges, triumphs, fears, and joys with other women. Over time, more and more women share their stories, maybe in a therapy group or over coffee. Eventually, they mentor other women, some start podcasts or circles that highlight women's voices. Those podcasts and circles become ripples in a much larger pond. The belief in the power of shared voices takes on a life of its own. One voice can make others brave. That collective power doesn't require grandeur or a megaphone, it requires presence, space, and the willingness to listen and lead together.

I started a women's circle with some of the women in my life. I wasn't sure how it would resonate, but boy was I surprised! These women all came to me and thanked me for starting the group. More than that, they shared so many intimate and impactful stories with one another and most of them did not know each other before the group. It was powerful and exhilarating for me.

A Real-Life Story: Tarana Burke and the Power of Amplification

I mentioned Tarana Burke in chapter four. But I think her story belongs here. The founder of the original *#MeToo* movement, she began her work long before it became a hashtag. As a youth worker in Alabama, Burke spent years listening to young girls share their experiences of sexual violence. Many of those girls had no language for what had happened to them, and no safe space to process it, let alone share it.

Burke's leadership was about making space for others to find their voices. She created support circles. She offered words when others had none. And when the #*MeToo* hashtag went viral years later, it wasn't just a cultural moment, it was a culmination of quiet, persistent work that had empowered thousands of women to speak up and be believed.

Her story reminds us that real change often begins in intimate spaces, community centers, classrooms, small circles of trust. Burke didn't seek the spotlight; she sought to share it with all women. And in doing so, she sparked one of the most transformative global conversations of our time.

The #*MeToo* movement ushered in a global reckoning around sexual harassment, abuse, and violence, creating space for survivors to speak out and be believed. But its momentum didn't stop there. In response to the widespread #*MeToo* stories of workplace misconduct and silence at the highest levels of power, the #*TimesUp* movement emerged, focused specifically on systemic change, accountability, and legal support to fight sexual harassment and advocate for gender parity in the workplace. While #*MeToo* lifted the veil, #*TimesUp* moved to challenge the structures that enabled harm, calling for a culture where women's voices don't just echo, they catalyze transformation.

This is the power of helping other women find their voices. It's not about leading them, it's about walking beside them until they remember they've had the power all along.

Story

I've attended many wealth management conferences over the years. Before the big DEI push of the Biden administration, I would attend high profile industry events. Most people being 50+ yo white males. I would often arrive early to the events and find a table to sit at. I was often avoided. The room would start to fill and people would intentionally avoid the table I was at unless there was no other space for them then they'd be forced to sit at my table. I met one of my closest advisor friends this way. I looked up and the only other empty table was his. He was a black male. We ended up doing a partner activity so we joined tables. This doesn't happen as much now but it happened several times in the early days.

Being unmuted isn't about speaking louder. It's about refusing to shrink. It's about advocating not just for yourself, but for others who are still being passed over in silence. I hope my story becomes an example not just for women, but for anyone who grew up thinking that wealth or success was for other people. I want them to see what's possible, and know they belong here too. I used to google women in my field for hope and proof that I belong. I hope over time we can create communities where no one has to search for proof that they belong as I once did and that every individual feels empowered to thrive.

Chapter 9:

Gender-Based Violence and Women as Victims

"Power and violence are opposites; where the one rules absolutely, the other is absent"
- Hannah Arendt

Violence against women is not just a person-al tragedy, it is a public crisis, a systemic failure, and a reflection of power structures that continue to minimize women's voices, bodies, and experiences while maintaining the power imbalance. Gender-based violence is one of the most pervasive human rights violations in the world, cutting across age, race, culture, geography, and socio-economic background.

While progress has been made in awareness and legislation, the reality remains stark. As I mentioned in chapter six, the statistics are staggering. According to the World Health Organization (WHO), 1 in 3 women globally has experienced physical and/or sexual violence in her lifetime, most often by an intimate partner. In the United States alone, the National Coalition Against Domestic Violence reports that nearly 20 people per minute are physically abused by an intimate partner. Over the course of a year, this equates to more than 10 million women and men.

Multiple studies show that women comprise the majority of those harmed. Lifetime prevalence rates estimate 1 in 3 women and 1 in 4 men experience intimate partner violence. In terms of annual harm, data indicates roughly 1.3 million women and 835,000 men report being raped or physically assaulted by a partner. Other estimates suggest the number of physical assaults reach 4.5 million against women and 2.9 million against men annually.

"Gender-based violence does not occur in a vacuum. It is shaped and sustained by cultural norms, unequal power dynamics, and institutional failures. From public harassment to systemic discrimination in legal proceedings, women are often retraumatized by the very systems that claim to protect them. And while this violence is most often directed at women and girls, it intersects with race, class, disability, sexuality, and immigration status in ways that deepen vulnerability and compound marginalization.

Globally, gender-based violence manifests in a range of forms:

- Child marriage: More than 12 million girls are married before the age of 18 every year, often facing abuse and denied education. Child marriage is legal in 37 states as of 2025.

- Honor-based violence: In some parts of the world, it is legal to kill or assault women who defied traditional norms around marriage, sexuality, or obedience.

- Sexual violence in conflict zones: Rape is routinely used as a weapon of war, intended to terrorize and destabilize entire communities.

- Online abuse: Women, particularly activists and public figures, face targeted digital harassment and threats, often of a sexually violent nature, and with little to no accountability.

- Maybe it's just me but why do we call it 'sexual assault' when it's actually rape?

- And, of course, domestic violence, which is overwhelmingly perpetrated against women.

This violence is political. It's cultural. And it's deeply personal.

Historical Context of Resistance

Women have always resisted violence, not just by surviving, but by organizing, advocacy, and cultural transformation. Movements like Take Back the Night, launched in the 1970s, created public spaces for women to protest sexual violence and reclaim their right to safety. In the 1990s, The Clothesline Project began displaying t-shirts made by survivors to publicly acknowledge and share their experiences.

More recently, as mentioned previously, the *#MeToo* movement, propelled globally in 2017, gave millions of women a way to speak their truth and hold perpetrators accountable. It exposed the scale of sexual harassment and violence for women of all ages, races, ethnicities, and socio-economic status, as well as every industry from Hollywood to hospitality. *#MeToo* forced institutions to respond.

Globally, women-led movements have sparked major reforms. As mentioned in chapter 1, in Argentina, the *Ni Una Menos*, ("Not One Less") movement mobilized against femicide and gender violence, demanding government accountability and cultural change. In India, mass protests following the widely publicized 2012 Delhi gang rape led to legislative reform and renewed conversations about women's safety.

These movements are not just moments of protest, they are declarations of power. They reveal the collective strength of women who refuse to be silenced. They demonstrate that voice is not only personal, but also political. And they remind us that even in the face of violence, women have found ways to rise.

I grew up during the National Organization for Women's heyday. Gloria Steinem and Betty Friedan were heroes of mine. I read the *Feminine Mystique*, used my babysitting money to pay for a subscription to Ms. magazine, and felt a kinship with the women behind these publications that I could not explain at the time. I just knew their voices echoed mine. Their words inspired me and filled me with conviction.

Domestic Violence: The Hidden Epidemic

Domestic violence, a specific form of gender-based violence, is both deeply personal and heartbreakingly common. It includes physical abuse, emotional manipulation, financial control, sexual violence, and psychological intimidation. At its core, domestic violence is about power and control. And too often, it is cloaked in silence.

Domestic violence is frequently hidden behind closed doors and normalized in communities. Victims are often silenced not only by their abusers but by the cultural, legal, and institutional systems that fail to protect or support them.

Statistics underscore the urgency:

- In the U.S., 1 in 4 women will experience severe intimate partner physical violence in her lifetime. The reality is that these numbers are only part of the truth. We know that intimate partner violence is one of the most underreported crimes worldwide.

- Intimate partners most commonly abuse women between the ages of 18–24.

- The presence of a gun in a domestic violence situation increases the risk of homicide by 500%.

- In the U.S., current or former male intimate partners perpetrate half of the murders where women are the victims.

- Murder is the leading cause of death among pregnant women in the United States.

These are not isolated incidents. They are part of a larger cultural narrative that conditions us to overlook, excuse, or rationalize violence against women.

Survivors face complex barriers to leaving abusive relationships, including economic dependence, fear of retaliation, lack of housing, and concern for their children. For women of color, immigrants, LGBTQ+ individuals, and disabled women, the barriers are compounded by racism, xenophobia, homophobia, and ableism. Abusive husbands are more than 2x as likely to seek sole custody of children. Meanwhile, judges grant sole or joint custody to 70% of fathers. The two statistics side by side would imply that in many instances, abusive fathers are granted custody. SO: when women speak up about their abuse or leave, they are risking losing their kids to an abuser. It is vital for women to use their voices to advocate for justice and equity, and the fact that it still often backfires on them highlights that the journey is ongoing and the choice is unbearable.

The voices of survivors are often questioned, doubted, or outright ignored. Sometimes, law enforcement retraumatizes them. Courts often fail them. And communities may shame or isolate them.

But when women break the silence around domestic violence, they do more than reclaim their own power, they ignite a cultural shift. Speaking out against abuse is a radical act of resistance. It challenges the systems that keep violence hidden and perpetrators protected. It changes the story for the next generation.

I don't want to portray women as victims, but rather acknowledge a reality too often swept aside. Until we address the roots and realities of domestic violence, we cannot fully redefine power. Because real power, the kind that liberates, does not coexist with violence. It demands safety, equity, and a voice for all.

This reminds me of the story circulating online that asks women a simple, chilling question: *If you were alone in the woods, would you rather run into a bear or an unknown man?*

Overwhelmingly, women answer: *the bear.*

It might sound absurd, until you pause to consider the truth behind the response. The bear is dangerous, yes. But its danger is honest. Predictable. The bear doesn't carry centuries of entitlement. It doesn't gaslight, stalk, harass, or harm in silence. It doesn't smile while doing it.

UNMUTED

The fact that so many women instinctively choose the bear reveals something raw and urgent: many of us have internalized the reality that men, even strangers, often pose a greater threat than nature itself. And that reality shapes how we walk through the world, through forests, city streets, corporate offices, relationships, and even our own homes.

After this story went viral, men were dumbfounded and some were outraged. Not outraged that women had reason to choose the bear (though there were many who were) but because they simply could not understand the concept of women's fear in this scenario. For me, that solidified one of the main reasons gender-based violence against women exists. Many men have a hard time thinking past their own egos when it comes to gender-based violence against women. Men insist we need them to protect us. When we ask, "protect us from what?" The answer is not from bears, but from other men!

Women explaining their choice of bear over men said things like, "If it's a bear, at least people will believe me." "If it's a bear, no one will ask me what I was wearing."

This story isn't just about fear. It's about the cost of not being believed, the exhaustion of navigating risk, and the unspoken ways women adapt to survive. And it's about why our collective voice matters. Because when we speak these truths out loud, when we stop gaslighting ourselves and each other, we shift the culture that tells us to be quiet, polite, and grateful to survive.

Cultural and Legal Silence

One of the most devastating aspects of gender-based violence is how often it is rendered invisible by the very systems meant to address it. Survivors are told not to "make a scene." They are warned not to ruin reputations. In too many cases, the pressure to stay silent is greater than the support for speaking out.

In 2015 a Stanford athlete forcibly assaulted an unconscious young woman behind a dumpster. There were two eyewitnesses.

Yet when the court's scale weighed her trauma against his future, it tipped in favor of the offender. "Twenty minutes of action" echoed in the public consciousness—crafted by his father—and transformed a violent crime into a regrettable lapse. Media coverage bowed to his pedigree, not her pain. She was left to absorb the message that speaking up meant destroying someone's life, even as they had destroyed hers.

Culturally, we've normalized harmful language, jokes about abuse, victim-blaming, or trivializing assault as a misunderstanding. In the media, perpetrators are often given more sympathy than survivors. In law, the burden of proof often rests with the victim, and justice can be agonizingly slow or out of reach altogether.

Even well-meaning communities may fail survivors by offering forgiveness over accountability or prioritizing reputations over justice. These dynamics teach women and girls early on that their pain is negotiable, that their safety is optional, and that their voices are secondary. As with the Stanford student in the above story, when a rapist's "bright future" is reason for a judge to let him off lightly, it ignores the compromised bright future of a traumatized woman who never gets justice or closure.

We must unlearn these narratives. When we talk about gender-based violence, we must also talk about systems, legal, cultural, religious, and familial, that uphold silence and disempowerment. The path forward must include accountability at every level: for individuals, for institutions, and for culture itself.

Normalized Harm: Everyday Dismissals That Mask Violence

One of the most dangerous aspects of gender-based violence is how easily it can be normalized. Comments like, "He's just protective," or "She's being dramatic," seem harmless on the surface but reflect deeper cultural narratives that excuse controlling behavior in men or minimize distress in women. These micro-dismissals accumulate over time, conditioning us to overlook or rationalize signs of abuse.

In workplaces, when men repeatedly interrupt women, it may well be laughed off as simply poor meeting etiquette. In a family, emotional manipulation may be disguised as love. These subtle cues reinforce the idea that discomfort, fear, or disrespect is something women should endure. As a result, many women struggle to even recognize their experience as abuse let alone feel empowered to name or confront it.

When harmful behavior is tolerated or disguised as care, it becomes harder to challenge and easier to excuse. Unlearning this conditioning begins with awareness and acknowledgment of how language, norms, and silence contribute to a culture that enables violence.

To live unmuted is to develop the ability to name these patterns, no matter how small. It's learning to say, "That made me uncomfortable," without apologizing. It's recognizing control masked as concern and setting a boundary anyway. And it's believing other women when they do the same.

Survivors Leading the Way: Healing, Advocacy, and Cultural Change

In the face of violence, many survivors do more than survive, they lead. They become peer counselors, authors, educators, and activists. They share their stories not only to heal, but to build a better future for others. From community centers to boardrooms, their voices shift policy, challenge bias, and humanize issues that statistics alone cannot.

Organizations like RAINN (Rape, Abuse & Incest National Network), the National Domestic Violence Hotline, and local women's shelters have been founded, staffed, and sustained by survivors and their allies. In these spaces, healing becomes a catalyst for change and solidarity becomes a form of leadership.

Public figures like Chanel Miller, mentioned in an earlier chapter, who courageously shared her victim impact statement after surviving sexual assault, have helped reframe the conversation around consent and accountability. Others, like Amanda Nguyen, who fought to reform laws around the rape kit backlog, demonstrate that even in the wake of trauma, survivors can and do drive meaningful change.

To support this shift, we must move beyond passive sympathy toward active solidarity. We must listen, believe, and uplift survivor voices not as tangential, but as central to redefining power. This is not just their work, it's all of ours.

Male Allies and the Responsibility of Change

While gender-based violence disproportionately affects women and girls (85% of domestic violence victims are women), dismantling it is not a task for women alone. Men have a critical role to play in transforming the culture that enables abuse. This starts with listening, truly listening, to the voices of survivors. But it must go further.

Men must examine how their own beliefs, behaviors, and silences may reinforce harm. They must be willing to speak up in locker rooms, boardrooms, and family rooms. They must challenge toxic masculinity, not just to protect women, but to liberate themselves from limiting roles that equate power with dominance.

Male allies in advocacy, education, and activism have helped broaden the conversation and shift responsibility. Groups like A Call to Men, Promundo, and MenEngage work with boys and men to promote healthy masculinity and prevent violence. Their work shows that redefining power includes everyone and that equity requires partnership, not pity.

The men who are confident and grounded in themselves are not threatened by women's voices. It is the insecure ones who panic. They may not call it fear, but that is what it is. Too many men are more invested in keeping the approval of other men—in locker rooms, boardrooms, and social spaces—than in standing beside women. These are the men I call *power adjacent*. They do not hold much power themselves, but they cling to its edges, hoping proximity will grant them status. In doing so, they sell out women, choosing male approval over integrity. Patriarchy was not built by strength. It was built both by dominant men who claimed power as their birthright and by the power-adjacent men who propped them up, hoping that by keeping women down they might gain a sliver of respect themselves.

Reimagining Safety: From Protection to Liberation

Too often, conversations around gender-based violence focus solely on protection, on teaching women to be vigilant, to defend themselves, to avoid danger. While self-defense and safety planning are important, they place the burden on the potential victims instead of the potential perpetrators.

True safety is not just the absence of danger, it's the presence of equity, respect, and freedom. It means forging systems, communities, and relationships in which women do not have to shrink, adapt, or armor themselves to survive. It means reimagining justice as something restorative and survivor centered, not just punitive.

Guarding against harm, creating the conditions in which harm is no longer normalized, is not true liberation. Liberation happens when we name the violence, believe survivors, and shift the balance of power so that all people, regardless of gender, can thrive.

Ending gender-based violence will not happen in silos. It will take collective accountability, cultural courage, and a refusal to accept silence as the norm. Together, we can create a world where safety is not a privilege but a right, and where power is no longer defined by control but by voice, dignity, and justice for all.

The Quiet Power of Resilience

Surviving violence is not just an act of endurance, it's an act of defiance. It is a refusal to be defined by someone else's cruelty or hurtfulness. The path of a survivor is often invisible to the outside world, quiet, nonlinear, full of both strength and sorrow. But it is within this path that we find one of the most powerful forces we possess: resilience.

Resilience is not the absence of struggle; it's the presence of determination. It's the decision to rebuild, to speak, to trust again. It's choosing to believe that your story matters even when others try to erase it. For women who have experienced gender-based violence, resilience looks like attending therapy, setting boundaries, advocating for others, or simply getting out of bed each morning with the weight of trauma still on their shoulders.

Resilience also disrupts the cycle. When one woman breaks her silence, she gives silent permission for others to do the same. When she claims her worth after years of being devalued, she shifts the energy of every space she enters. And when she speaks, she invites others to listen to themselves, to their pain, to their power.

What's remarkable is that this resilience often shows up long before we name it. Resilience is present in the decisions we make to protect ourselves, the hope we hold for something better, in the voice we begin to reclaim. It's not always loud or visible, but it's always there, waiting to be honored.

To live unmuted after violence is about more than recovery. It's about reinvention. It's about writing a new chapter, not in spite of what happened, but because we deserve to define what happens next.

Story

I was defending a client who was charged with lying/perjury at a DMV hearing. After a jury trial with my client testifying, the jury found my client not guilty. They believed the defendant's testimony. After the verdict was read, I went into the judge's chambers where he and the District Attorney (male) were snickering. This judge, who was from the south said in his southern drawl, "well Miss Johnson I hope your client didn't pull the wool over your eyes. I hope you didn't believe him because he was guilty, guilty, guilty." And he and the District Attorney began snickering again. I said "Judge he was just found not guilty by 12 other people who sat on the jury. And legally he is not guilty." The judge just looked at the DA with a wide grin and turned to me and said "awww you poor girl." He looked at me with such pity for believing my client.

It wasn't that his words or actions were so terrible (although legally unethical), it was the knowledge that he would have never said that to a male attorney. He was positioning himself as the father figure, completely paternalistic and at the same time intellectually superior.

STORY

I was working at a courthouse in California and the building was under construction. I happened to be going through a gate when the judge who was presiding at the court walked out of his office. I walked through the gate, and the judge gave me this very flirty smile. When I walked to where he was to go into the courthouse he continued to smile and told me, "Miss Johnson you look mighty fine hanging off that gate." I had no words and at that time although I felt violated, there was really nothing I could say. (It would of course be different now). But at that time, I felt I had to smile and play along. He was the judge and through me he could penalize my clients because of my actions.

These were two examples of many where men in higher positions than mine said unacceptable things to me that they would have never said to a male. I believe I had also learned that I should smile and joke back and take these things as a compliment or paternal care. Even though they felt nothing like that.

I wish in both instances I had pointed out that what these men were doing and saying was not caring or a compliment, but a way to be disrespectful to my position and my intellect.

Chapter 10:

The Global Struggle for Women's Freedom

"She remembered who she was and the game changed."
– Lalah Delia

Women around the world have long been subjected to systems of oppression that seek to control their bodies, silence their voices, and limit their choices. These systems are rooted in patriarchy, a cultural, religious, political, and economic structure that privileges male authority and seeks to maintain power through dominance and control.

In many places, women are still denied basic rights such as education, mobility, and political representation. Cultural and religious justifications are often used to reinforce these restrictions, and punishment for defiance can be swift and severe. The consequences of challenging these norms can range from social ostracism to imprisonment, violence, or death.

Oppression functions through both visible and invisible forces. It's woven into laws and policies, but also into social norms, expectations, and roles. It tells women that to be good is to be quiet, to be strong is to endure silently, and to be successful is to be pleasing. This conditioning starts early, shaping how girls view their worth and how women navigate the world. And it is reinforced by those who benefit from women's silence.

Women don't want to be men. The struggle isn't about replacing one form of dominance with another, it's about liberation. It's about having the freedom to choose, to speak, to lead, and to love without needing permission, or being punished for claiming that freedom. It's about recognizing our humanity without qualifiers or compromises.

Nowhere is this more starkly evident than in Iran and Afghanistan. In Iran, women have been at the forefront of protest movements, risking their lives to push back against a regime that mandates strict dress codes, limits their access to public spaces, and violently represses dissent. The death of Mahsa Amini in 2022, after Iran's morality police detained her, sparked a wave of nationwide and global protests, with women publicly removing their hijabs in defiance of the state's control. These protests have evolved into broader calls for freedom and civil rights, signaling a powerful resistance that continues despite brutal crackdowns.

In Afghanistan, the return of the Taliban to power in 2021 has led to a devastating rollback of women's rights. Girls are banned from attending school beyond the sixth grade, women are prohibited from most forms of employment, and female visibility in public life has been all but erased. Yet Afghan women continue to resist, teaching in underground schools, protesting at great personal risk, and speaking out on social media and international platforms. In many parts of Afghanistan women are prohibited from seeing male doctors and women can no longer study midwifery or practice healthcare. It begs the question, "What happens when all the women die from untreated health issues?"

The struggle for autonomy is not exclusive to other nations. Here in the United States, we are facing a different but no less significant form of restriction and subjugation. The Supreme Court's 2022 decision overturning Roe v. Wade marked a profound shift, stripping away hard-won federal protection for reproductive rights and signaling a broader rollback of bodily autonomy and specialized healthcare. It also raised urgent questions about privacy and equality. The decision didn't just revoke federal protection, it reignited a global conversation about the fragile nature of women's rights, even in countries that portray themselves as champions of freedom.

At the same time, cultural undercurrents like the rise of the "manosphere" and hyper-masculine "bruh" culture are resurfacing regressive narratives that women should be seen and not heard and are valued primarily for their ability to bear children or support men. Though less visible than in some parts of the world, these dynamics represent a steady erosion of freedoms once fought hard for and remind us that silence, here too, comes at a cost. These examples remind us that oppression is not passive, it is enforced, often violently. But they also remind us that resistance is equally powerful. When women in Iran chant "Women, Life, Freedom," or when Afghan girls attend secret schools under threat of death, they are not only fighting for themselves, they are courageously fighting on behalf of women everywhere.

The U.S. experience underscores an important truth: the permanence of progress is not guaranteed. Rights must be defended and reasserted with every generation. The erosion of reproductive rights here mirrors the mechanisms of control used elsewhere, restricting choices, silencing dissent, and undermining the agency of women under the guise of law or morality. Do what we say or you could die. We will let you die.

Oppression persists because it works to uphold the status quo. But change happens when women rise, resist, and refuse to be muted, whether in Tehran, Kabul, or Texas. The stories may differ in form, but the essence of the struggle is the same: women are not asking for power, they are claiming the right to their own lives, on their own terms. A right that is not anyone else's to give or take away.

While our voices are strong and powerful, we need men to stand beside us in support, and to use their voices as well. As I said before, we're not looking to be men, we are looking for men to be in solidarity with us. But we will fight the fight with or without them. If I sound angry, it's because I am. In the words of Greta Thunberg "We need more angry women!"

Religious Control and Interpretation

Another deeply rooted mechanism of control lies in the interpretation and enforcement of religious doctrine. Across many cultures, religion is used not only as a spiritual framework but as a political and social tool to enforce patriarchal authority.

In many Muslim-majority countries, for instance, conservative interpretations of Sharia law have been used to justify restrictions on women's dress, mobility, and legal rights. Yet within these same traditions, there are growing movements of Muslim women scholars and activists who are reclaiming space and challenging patriarchal interpretations. Organizations like Musawah and figures like Dr. Amina Wadud, an African-American convert to Islam, have been instrumental in advocating for gender justice within an Islamic framework. While Dr. Wadud is a lightning rod for both criticism and support, she nonetheless is using her voice to challenge norms and patriarchal interpretations of religious traditions.

In Christianity, women have historically been excluded from formal leadership roles, particularly in Catholicism and many evangelical denominations. Yet, movements like the Women's Ordination Conference and the increasing leadership of women in progressive Christian communities are challenging the notion that spiritual authority belongs to men alone.

In Hindu traditions, goddesses are revered and celebrated, yet in practice, many women face domestic and societal limitations. Reformist thinkers and female spiritual leaders are increasingly calling for a return to the inclusive and egalitarian roots of these traditions.

What unites these efforts is the demand for agency, the right to interpret and live with faith on one's own terms, as well as the right to provide faith-based leadership alongside men. Religion can be a source of strength and purpose, but when used to justify subjugation, it becomes another weapon in the arsenal of oppression. Women around the world are not rejecting faith, they are reclaiming it and reinterpreting it through a non-patriarchal lens.

Economic Control as a Tool of Oppression

A crucial but often overlooked form of control is economic oppression. Women's financial dependence on men has long been used as a silent enforcer of inequality, limiting women's choices, restricting their freedom, and undermining their autonomy.

Globally, women earn approximately 77 cents for every dollar earned by men. In many countries, women are still legally restricted from owning property, inheriting land, or accessing credit. In rural areas of sub-Saharan Africa and South Asia, for example, women often work the land but have no legal rights to it, leaving them vulnerable to displacement and exploitation.

In some regions, women are denied the ability to work at all. Even in wealthier nations like the United States, women face significant barriers to career advancement, are underrepresented in leadership, and usually bear the brunt of unpaid caregiving responsibilities. These economic disparities are not just statistics; they are structural tools of control.

In the United States, it wasn't until the 1970s that women were legally able to open a bank account, own property, or apply for credit without their husband's signature. The Equal Credit Opportunity Act of 1974 made it illegal to deny credit based on gender, but the societal impacts of decades of financial dependence still linger.

Economic control can also be subtle and personal. In relationships where one partner earns significantly more or controls the finances, power imbalances can quickly emerge. For women earning less or not working outside the home, access to money can become a point of vulnerability especially in abusive relationships. Conversely, when a woman earns more than her partner, she may face resentment, guilt, or pressure to downplay her success to maintain harmony.

Economic empowerment is directly tied to vocal empowerment. When women control their income, they are more likely to speak up at home, participate in political processes, and leave abusive situations. All reasons why, in my opinion, we still make far less than men for the same job. Microfinance initiatives, women-led cooperatives, and entrepreneurship programs have shown that when women have financial independence, their communities thrive. Economic power enables women to invest in education, healthcare, and civic engagement, strengthening not only their own position but that of future generations.

True liberation requires more than legal rights; it requires the resources to exercise those rights. As long as women remain financially constrained, their voices and their choices remain limited. Economic freedom is not a luxury. It is a prerequisite for equality, dignity, and the unmuted life.

Reimagining Domestic Labor: What If the System Were Reversed?

Imagine if every hour a woman spent cooking, cleaning, caregiving, scheduling, supporting, and managing emotional labor at home was counted as billable work. Now imagine if, instead of being invisible, this work required formal compensation, direct payments from her partner into an account she alone could access. What if, on top of that, her partner was required to contribute to her 401(k), recognizing her labor as crucial economic input?

This mental exercise forces us to confront the vast disparity in how we value labor. Domestic work, so often labeled "women's work," is the invisible scaffolding holding up households, economies, and entire societies. Yet it's rarely counted, rarely paid, and rarely respected.

What would shift if women had financial autonomy not dependent on their partner's generosity or goodwill? What if stay-at-home mothers and unpaid caregivers had the same financial security as salaried employees? What if marriage or partnership came with the legal and cultural recognition that unpaid labor is not free labor? And what about mothers with full-time jobs outside of the home who still do the majority of in-home work—how can they receive compensation and recognition?

This is not about reversing power, it's about redistributing respect and equity. If the roles were flipped, the imbalance would be instantly glaring. The thought of men needing "permission" to access money they didn't earn, or being expected to serve without acknowledgement, would be outrageous. And yet, for many women, it's simply life.

This exercise is not just a thought experiment, it's a call to imagine a future where domestic work is dignified, compensated, and no longer taken for granted. Because when we start valuing women's contributions in all spheres, not just the workplace, we shift the power paradigm in every home, every relationship, and every society.

Educational Access and the Suppression of Information

Education is one of the most powerful tools of liberation, yet it is often the first target of oppressive regimes. Denying women and girls access to education is a deliberate tactic used to maintain control, limit opportunities, and suppress dissent.

In countries like Afghanistan and Pakistan, girls face significant obstacles to completing even primary education. According to UNESCO, nearly 130 million girls worldwide are out of school. When girls are denied education, they are more vulnerable to child marriage, exploitation, and poverty. A lack of education limits their access to information, healthcare, and civic participation, reinforcing cycles of dependency and silence.

Even in countries with formal access to education, disparities persist. Curricula often lack representation of women's achievements and voices, and educational environments can perpetuate gender bias through both content and classroom dynamics. Girls may be discouraged from pursuing STEM fields, silenced in discussions, or penalized for assertiveness.

Information suppression extends beyond schooling. In the digital age, access to online resources, uncensored media, and social networks is crucial for awareness and advocacy. Yet many women face digital harassment, censorship, or surveillance that chills speech and activism.

Liberation requires knowledge and knowledge demands access. When women are educated and informed, they gain the tools to question injustice, advocate for their rights, and support others in doing the same. Ensuring educational and informational access is not just an act of inclusion, it is a revolutionary step toward dismantling oppression.

In the United States, we are witnessing a quiet but deliberate restriction of educational access both in what is taught and who gets to learn. Banned books, sanitized curricula, and legislation limiting honest conversations about race, gender, and history are reshaping the educational landscape. At the same time, access to higher education is becoming increasingly out of reach, especially for low-income and marginalized communities. Rising tuition costs, student debt burdens, and reduced funding for public universities are barriers that disproportionately affect women, particularly women of color.

This is compounded by policies like the overturning of Roe v. Wade, which limits reproductive autonomy and forces many young women into life-altering decisions before they've had the chance to fully pursue education or career paths. When you strip away access to both knowledge and choice, you control not only a woman's present but her entire future. You also, by extension, create positive generational effects for that woman's extended family and descendants. Let's call it what it is – forced birth.

Digital Resistance & Social Media Movements

Social media has become one of the most potent tools for women challenging systems of oppression around the world. It functions as a modern-day megaphone, amplifying voices that have long been silenced and connecting women across borders to share strategies, stories, and solidarity.

In addition to the previously mentioned *Ni Una Menos* digital movement, in Iran, the hashtag *#MahsaAmini* became a rallying cry after the death of a 22-year-old Kurdish woman who was arrested by Iran's morality police in 2022 for allegedly wearing her hijab improperly and later died in custody under disputed circumstances. Her death ignited widespread protests across Iran and beyond, uniting people under the slogan "Woman, Life, Freedom." The hashtag galvanized global outrage and support, providing a platform for activists, artists, and ordinary citizens to bear witness and demand justice. Videos of women cutting their hair in protest, chanting in the streets, and resisting with acts of everyday courage flooded timelines and newsfeeds, making it impossible for the world to look away.

In the U.S., the *#MeToo* movement gained explosive traction in 2017 as millions of women shared their stories of sexual harassment and assault. What followed was a seismic shift in how institutions address misconduct, power dynamics, and accountability.

These digital uprisings are more than hashtags; they are revolutions in real time. They are redefining what resistance looks like in the digital age: decentralized, intersectional, and impossible to silence. By sharing their truths and rallying others to action, women are building global networks of support that challenge not just individual injustices, but the very structures that allow them to persist. There is strength in numbers and knowing that you are not alone in the battle.

The digital sphere is not without its risks, though. Trolls, threats, and surveillance are real dangers, but it remains a critical space where women can be seen, heard, and joined in their fight.

Whether in hashtags or livestreams, the collective voice of women continues to echo across borders, demanding a world where freedom and dignity are non-negotiable.

Social media has given women a megaphone that cannot easily be taken away. Voices once confined to private whispers are now amplified to millions, sparking movements, shifting culture, and refusing to be ignored. Yet with that power has come a ferocious backlash. The more women speak, the louder the pushback becomes—men panicking at the loss of control, responding with rage, harassment, and threats meant to force us back into silence. This backlash is real, and it is dangerous. But it is also proof of impact. When women's voices rise, the ground shakes. We cannot minimize the risks, but neither can we let them silence us. To be unmuted means speaking anyway, with the knowledge that every word carries both risk and the possibility of transformation.

Intersectionality: Class, Race, and Geography

Oppression does not look the same for every woman. As mentioned in chapter 6, Kimberlé Crenshaw's concept of intersectionality helps us understand how race, class, gender identity, sexuality, disability, and geographic location intersect to shape unique experiences of discrimination and access.

A Black woman in Mississippi will navigate a different set of systemic obstacles than a white woman in New York. For example, she faces disparities in healthcare, wage equity, policing, and educational access. Challenges that are compounded, not because she is a woman or Black, but because she is both.

Similarly, a Dalit woman in rural India lives at the intersection of caste, gender, and poverty. Her struggle for dignity includes resistance against both patriarchal norms and a deeply entrenched caste system. Her reality is shaped by multiple layers of marginalization, requiring a movement that sees and addresses the full scope of her identity.

Indigenous women, migrant women, trans women, and women with disabilities all bring different truths to the table. Their stories are not sidebars to the feminist movement, they are central to it. Equity can only be achieved when we center those most impacted by oppression and allow their voices to lead the way.

Intersectionality reminds us that solidarity requires more than shared identity. It requires a willingness to listen, to learn, and to make space for difference, not just in theory, but in practice.

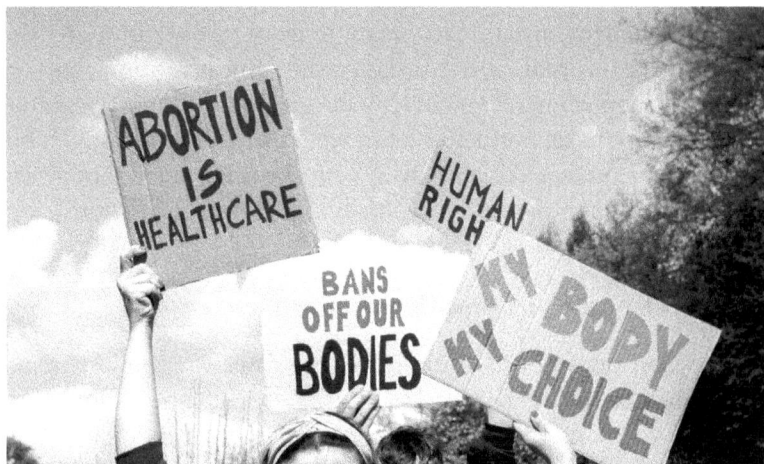

Resistance in Art, Literature, and Music

Throughout history, when traditional platforms have been inaccessible or unsafe, women have turned to the arts to voice dissent, reclaim narratives, and mobilize communities. The arts are not merely decorative or for pleasure, they are often deeply political, especially when created by those whose voices have been marginalized.

In Iran, where public protests are often brutally suppressed, women have used underground music and poetry as vehicles for resistance. Songs banned by the government circulate online, carrying powerful messages of defiance and unity. These creative acts become a form of protest that reaches both domestic and global audiences.

In Latin America, feminist street art has exploded across cities in the form of vibrant murals, wheat-paste posters, and stenciled slogans. These artworks often depict women rising, resisting, and reimagining a world free of femicide and systemic abuse. Groups like "Mujeres Grabando Resistencias" in Argentina blend art and activism to raise awareness and claim public space.

Across borders, women writers from banned Iranian poets to Indigenous authors in North America, have used literature as resistance. Their stories offer counter-narratives to dominant systems of power and keep cultural memory alive. These works often face censorship but persist through underground distribution and global translation networks.

Art, music, and literature are powerful tools not only for individual expression but for collective transformation. They allow women to bear witness, spark dialogue, and inspire movements. In every era and across every culture, these creative expressions have reminded the world: we are here, we are watching, and we will not be silenced.

I recently sent my daughter a video of Helen Reddy's anthem "I Am Woman" and told her it was my call to action as a teenager. She replied with two of her own: Emmy Meli's "I Am Woman" and Paris Paloma's haunting "Labour." On the one hand, it saddens me that we still need these anthems decades later.

But on the other, it fills me with hope to see the next generation picking up the torch, louder, bolder, and more united than ever. There's nothing like music and art to bring people together and energize a movement.

Hope and Global Solidarity

Across borders and belief systems, women are rising not just for themselves, but for one another. From solidarity marches in the wake of gender-based violence to cross-cultural feminist conferences and online platforms for collective action, a global sisterhood is forming.

International Women's Day events, the Women's March, and previously mentioned grassroots campaigns like *#NiUnaMenos* and *#MahsaAmini* show that resistance is not confined by geography. These movements signal that women's struggles and victories are deeply interconnected. What affects one of us affects us all.

In places like India, Argentina, Kenya, and the U.S., local efforts to promote reproductive justice, end femicide, and increase access to education are now linked through networks of global advocacy. Feminist organizations are partnering across borders to exchange tools, amplify voices, and push for lasting legislative and cultural change.

This chapter ends not in despair, but in hope. Because while the structures of oppression are vast, so is our collective voice. When we speak, march, create, and connect, we are not just resisting, we are reimagining the world. We continue to explore what it means to live unmuted to name hard truths, to build communities of care and accountability, and to co-create a world where every woman can live, lead, and love without fear.

And we're doing it together.

Story

My wife Andrea was in labor and could tell she was nearly ready to push. The doctor stopped by on the way to another birth to tell her she was wrong. "You have at least two more hours before you'll need to push." The doctor said she'd be back after two more deliveries and to "hang on." Twelve minutes later, Andrea was fully dilated and the baby was coming. It became clear that something was wrong, but the doctor did not show up until urgently paged. The cord was double wrapped around my baby daughter's neck and she nearly died. It took a team of doctors and nurses to save the baby's life while Andrea, traumatized, could only watch as I held her.

Two weeks later, I took Andrea and the baby to see a therapist in the same practice as their OB. Andrea was suffering from debilitating anxiety that alternated with horrible depression. She backed away from people who tried to talk to her, compulsively ran her fingernails down her neck over and over again in an unconscious gesture, and stopped eating and sleeping. They found out that Andrea was suffering from PTSD too. The therapist gave us exercises she could do to reduce anxiety—holding her hands in ice water, counting from 100 to 0 by sevens, bending over to hold her ankles in a hot shower. Andrea did all of them, but they did not touch her symptoms.

Things were escalating and Andrea was no longer functioning. I was beside myself, completely out of my depth and unable to help her. Rather than referring Andrea to a reproductive psychiatrist (an expert in perinatal mental health), her OB prescribed Zoloft and said to wait two weeks for it to work. But no one had taken a thorough psychiatric medical history. If they had, they'd know that Zoloft is contraindicated for people with a family history of bipolar disorder. It can make things worse. Andrea had several close relatives with a bipolar diagnosis.

And, for Andrea, things quickly got much worse on the Zoloft. Her symptoms ramped up and she began having suicidal thoughts and signs of psychosis, including paranoia and hearing phantom sounds, like baby cries, even when the baby was sound asleep. We toughed out the two weeks trusting that the medication would begin to work as the doctor had promised. It did not.

Desperate, we sought help from anyone who might consider a different medication. And soon, Andrea was telling me and every doctor we saw that she needed to be hospitalized. She did not see any alternative, aside from ending her life, to make it all stop.

We saw 7 different psychiatrists at 7 different hospitals and were told essentially the same thing each time. Taking one look at her—a privileged, attractive woman with a supportive husband—and hearing her say, "I'm in trouble. I feel crazy," their response was, "No you're not."

Not one of these psychiatrists had the understanding of maternal mental health, which I now understand is a specialty that is hugely under-represented in the field, to realize what was happening. Even though she was telling them, very clearly, in words not difficult to understand: "I am afraid I'm going to end my life if something doesn't change," no one listened. She explained that as a woman of faith she was terrified that she'd go to hell if she did what she wanted to do. Could they please help her?

"Stop worrying. Go home. Take a hot bath. Talk to your friends. You'll be fine." When she begged to be admitted, they said, "You're not like them," meaning the people being treated in the psych wards. At one clinic, almost the last on our list, we arrived before anyone else at 8:00 a.m. but were made to wait all day. At 4:00 we were the only ones left in the waiting room. That's when we found out that the psychiatrist had gone home without seeing us. He had scoffed at his receptionist when he found out we had arrived in a Mercedes.

The last doctor we went to see took me aside. He said, "Listen. She's not like the people in our ward. She'll be fine. Women like your wife will never want to be remembered not looking their best, so they use pills or they go in the garage and start the car. Here's what you do if you're worried. Take away the pills and car keys. It'll be fine."

Forty-one days after she gave birth to our beautiful daughter, she hung herself. I lost my beloved wife and our daughter never knew her mother.

Suicide is the leading cause of death in new mothers. Maybe it's time for people to listen to them.

Chapter Eleven:

The Fight Continues – Unmuted in the Now

"I am no longer accepting the things I cannot change.
I am changing the things I cannot accept."
-Angela Davis

We do not live in a post-patriarchal world. We live in a moment where the women's rights we once assumed to be secure are again being questioned, challenged, and in some cases, stripped away.

Across the U.S., the conversation around women's rights has shifted from quiet concern to urgent alarm. The overturning of *Roe v. Wade* not only stripped women of their federal right to make decisions about their own bodies, it sent a message. A message that women's autonomy is still up for debate. The lesson? Progress is never permanent. It must be protected, spoken for, and sometimes, reclaimed.

Now, in 2025, under the current administration, the tension is palpable. While there are those in power fighting for equality and restoration of rights, there is also a sharp rise in political rhetoric that seeks to silence, shame, and suppress. Bills targeting reproductive healthcare, restrictions on gender-affirming care, and ongoing debates over access to education, employment protections and workplace harassment protections all echo a broader cultural attempt to put women back in their place—a place chosen for them by the patriarchy. We, the 51%, understand the role still—and again—being chosen for us. To be quiet, compliant, and controlled. Well, we, the 51%--reject it.

Because women are not going back.

We are not just reacting. We are organizing. We are running for office. We are building coalitions. We are reclaiming our narratives, our bodies, our futures. We are using our voices louder, bolder, and more unapologetically than ever before.

To be unmuted now is to recognize that the personal is political. That your story, your choice, your boundaries, and your leadership are acts of resistance. And they matter more than ever.

This book has explored how women silence themselves, how society silences them, and how they break free. But we cannot separate the individual from the collective. And right now, the collective needs your voice. It needs your vote, your advocacy, your mentorship, your storytelling. Because this moment in history is not just a chapter in your life, it's a chapter in our shared legacy.

I, for one, am saddened and disgusted that we must once again fight for our rights. I am horrified for my daughter, who now has fewer rights over her body than I did at her age.

The fight for women's rights isn't over. But we are not starting from silence. We are starting from strength.

Undermining Access: How Higher Education Is Being Subverted for Women

While the erosion of women's rights often makes headlines around reproductive healthcare, the quieter dismantling of access to higher education is just as concerning and deeply connected. In recent years, policy shifts, funding cuts, and ideological restrictions have begun to reshape the educational landscape in ways that disproportionately impact women, particularly those from marginalized communities.

At the heart of this trend is a growing political movement to limit academic freedom and censor curricula related to gender studies, race, sexuality, and social justice. Bills have been introduced or passed in several states to ban or restrict these fields, targeting the very frameworks that help young women understand systemic inequality, develop critical thinking skills, and find their voices in a world that often tries to silence them.

This isn't just about ideology, it's about control. When women are denied access to information, they are less equipped to challenge the systems that oppress them. When colleges and universities are pressured to eliminate programs that center equity and inclusion, it sends a broader message: Your truth does not belong here. In fact, your truth is not truth at all. This is the effect of these deletions and alterations that will burden us for decades to come.

But it goes further still. Rising tuition costs, the rollback of student debt forgiveness programs, and efforts to eliminate diversity-focused scholarships have created new financial and structural barriers. For many women, especially first-generation college students, single mothers, or women of color, these policies mean the difference between pursuing a degree or being forced into early motherhood, minimum wage work, or economic dependency.

The correlation is clear: reduce access to higher education, restrict reproductive freedom, and you reinforce a cycle that eradicates women's autonomy. You mute voices before they've had the chance to speak.

In this climate, advocacy for educational access is not separate from the fight for women's rights; it is integral to it. To be unmuted is to push back against this oppression. To demand more than survival. To insist that women and girls have not only the right to speak, but the right to learn, to question, and to lead.

From Outrage to Action

It's easy to feel overwhelmed. The pace of regression in women's rights, from healthcare to workplace protections to educational access, can be dizzying. But we cannot let exhaustion become silence. We cannot let outrage dissolve into apathy. Now is the time to turn our unmuted voices into unrelenting action.

Being unmuted doesn't always mean marching or megaphones, though those can be powerful tools. It can also mean showing up in quieter, consistent ways:

- **Mentor a woman rising behind you.** Pass down the tools, language, and confidence that helped you survive and thrive.

- **Vote in every election.** From local school boards to the presidency—every race holds the potential to protect or erode our rights.

- **Support reproductive justice organizations** doing the work on the ground, especially those led by women of color.

- **Disrupt harmful narratives in everyday conversations.** When someone jokes, minimizes, or misrepresents, speak up. Even a single sentence can make a difference.

- **Build spaces of belonging.** Whether in your workplace, your community, or your circle of friends, create cultures where women are safe to speak, lead, and live authentically.

- **Run for local office.** Fill the school boards and the town councils. Women in those leadership positions can pave the way for more women leaders to make it to elected positions in Congress, governorships and dare I say...the presidency.

Unmuting the Next Generation

We owe it to the next generation to be louder than the forces trying to pull us back. What we normalize today becomes the foundation for what our daughters, nieces, and mentees believe is possible. If we model self-silencing, perfectionism, or disempowerment, they'll inherit that. If we model self-trust, boundary-setting, advocacy, and truth-telling, they'll inherit that too.

Let's leave them a world where being female is not a liability. Where "leadership" and "woman" are synonymous. Where justice is not aspirational, it's expected, and delivered.

This is Not the End - It's the Inheritance

You are part of a lineage of women who have resisted, persisted, and redefined power with every generation. From suffragists to civil rights leaders, from the women of *#MeToo* and *#TimesUp* to the teenagers organizing walkouts today, you are standing on shoulders, and you are becoming someone else's shoulder too.

This is not the end of the story. It's the inheritance. The torch you carry now is lit by every woman who came before you. What you do with it is your legacy.

So let us be clear:

Your voice is not too much.

Your anger is not too loud.

Your dreams are not too big.

Your leadership is not too late.

Do not ask for permission. Instead, set the terms.

Unmuted is not just a book title. It is a declaration. A way of being. A way of leading. And it is how we will write the next chapter in history together.

CONCLUSION: YOU ARE THE REDEFINITION

*"I am grateful to be a woman. I must have
done something great in another life."*
— Maya Angelou

You are not waiting for power. You *are* power.

Every story in these pages, every truth unearthed, every voice reclaimed has pointed to this: the future is not something handed down from above. It is co-created by women who no longer wait for permission. Women who speak, who rise, who refuse to shrink.

Your story is not small. It's not "just personal." It is part of a larger movement. One that spans generations and geographies, one that reverberates in boardrooms and classrooms, kitchens and courthouses. Every time you tell the truth, set a boundary, speak with courage, or lift another woman's voice, you redefine what leadership, power, and progress look like.

Power won't be handed to us. We must claim it, in the ways only we can.

The act of finding and using your voice is more than personal. It's transformative. Every step you've taken to unlearn silence is a step toward reshaping the world. Not in sweeping declarations, but in the everyday choices to show up fully, lead with integrity, and live without apology.

You are part of a larger story, one that's still being written by women everywhere. A story of courage, connection, disruption, and redefinition. The kind of power you carry isn't loud for the sake of volume. It's clear because it's rooted in truth.

So, take up space. Use your voice. Trust your gut. Ask the hard questions. Rewrite the old rules. And when it gets hard, remember you are not alone. You are part of something bigger. We rise louder, braver, and freer together.

Speak the words that feel most real. Lead in ways that feel aligned with who you are, not who you were told to be. Your voice isn't just an instrument of change, it is change.

And remember: the future is being shaped right now by you, and by all of us who are choosing to live unmuted.

Lead boldly. Live unapologetically. Speak, and keep speaking—until the world listens.

Unmute your life. Speak with purpose, act with conviction, and lead with heart. In boardrooms, classrooms, living rooms, or courtrooms, your voice carries weight. Use it. The world won't change because we whisper. It will change because we *insist*.

Reflection Prompts

Where in your life have you stayed silent to keep the peace, and what might become possible if you chose to speak instead?

Write a letter to the next generation. What do you want them to know about voice, power, and what it means to live unmuted?

References

World Health Organization. (2021). Violence against women: Prevalence estimates, 2018 (Global and regional estimates of violence against women) [PDF]. Geneva: WHO.

World Health Organization. (2024). Violence against women [Fact sheet]. Retrieved from https://www.who.int/news-room/fact-sheets/detail/violence-against-women

UNICEF. (2024, October 10). Over 370 million girls and women globally subjected to rape or sexual assault as children [Press release]. Retrieved from https://www.unicef.org/press-releases/over-370-million-girls-and-women-globally-subjected-rape-or-sexual-assault-children

UN Women. (2024, November). Femicides in 2023: Global estimates of intimate partner/family-related femicides (Research brief). New York: UN Women. Retrieved from https://www.unwomen.org/sites/default/files/2024-11/femicides-in-2023-global-estimates-of-intimate-partner-family-member-femicides-en.pdf

UN Women. (2024, November 22). One woman or girl is killed every 10 minutes by their intimate partner or family member – new UNODC and UN Women data shows [Press release]. Retrieved from https://www.unwomen.org/en/news-stories/press-release/2024/11/one-woman-or-girl-is-killed-every-10-minutes-by-their-intimate-partner-or-family-member

Black, M. C., Basile, K. C., Breiding, M. J., Smith, S. G., Walters, M. L., Merrick, M. T., Chen, J., & Stevens, M. R. (2011). The National Intimate Partner and Sexual Violence Survey (NISVS): 2010 Summary Report. Atlanta, GA: National Center for Injury

Prevention and Control, Centers for Disease Control and Prevention.

Cheng, M., & Horon, I. (2010). Intimate-partner homicide among pregnant and postpartum women. Obstetrics & Gynecology, 115(6), 1181–1186. https://doi.org/10.1097/AOG.0b013e3181df94f8

Tahirih Justice Center. (2025, April). Ending child marriage, state by state [Policy brief]. Retrieved from https://www.tahirih.org/wp-content/uploads/2025/04/Child-Marriage-in-the-States-Two-Pager.pdf

UNFPA. (n.d.). Child marriage [Web page]. Retrieved from https://www.unfpa.org/child-marriage

Villacampa, C. (2024). Honour-based violence: Legal and institutional frameworks and gaps. Women's Studies International Forum. Retrieved from [ScienceDirect]

United Nations Office on Drugs and Crime. (n.d.). Gender-related killing of women and girls [eBook]. Retrieved from https://www.unodc.org/documents/justice-and-prison-reform/GRK_eBook.pdf

Amnesty International. (1999). Violence Against Women in the Name of Honour (Report). London: Amnesty International.

UN Women / UNIFEM. (n.d.). Rape as a tactic of war [Factsheet]. Retrieved from https://www.unwomen.org/sites/default/files/Headquarters/Media/Publications/UNIFEM/EVAWkit_06_Factsheet_ConflictAndPostConflict_en.pdf

Wood, E. J. (2018). Rape as a practice of war: Toward a typology of political violence. In United Nations, Sexual Violence in Conflict: United Nations Action. Retrieved from https://www.un-.org/sexualviolenceinconflict/wp-content/uploads/2019/05/report/rape-as-a-practice-of-war-toward-a-typology-of-political-violence/wood-PS-2018-rape-as-a-practice-of-war.pdf

Watson, S. (2023). Online abuse of women: An interdisciplinary scoping review. Journal of Gender Studies. Retrieved from https://www.tandfonline.com/doi/full/10.1080/14680777.2023.2181136

Brady: United Against Gun Violence. (n.d.). Domestic violence and guns [Web page]. Retrieved from https://www.bradyunited.org/resources/issues/domestic-violence-and-guns-2

AbiNader, M. A., et al. (2023). Examining intimate partner violence-related fatalities. Journal of Family Violence. Retrieved from https://www.ncbi.nlm.nih.gov/pmc/articles/PMC9838333/

Lawn, R. B., & Koenen, K. C. (2022). Homicide is a leading cause of death for pregnant women in the US. The BMJ. https://doi.org/10.1136/bmj.o2499

Wallace, M. E., Gillispie-Bell, V., Cruz, K., Davis, K., & Vilda, D. (2021). Homicide during pregnancy and the postpartum period in the United States, 2018–2019. Obstetrics & Gynecology. https://www.ncbi.nlm.nih.gov/pmc/articles/PMC9134264/

www.ingramcontent.com/pod-product-compliance
Lightning Source LLC
Chambersburg PA
CBHW051738020426
42333CB00014B/1363